TEACHER'S PET PUBLICATIONS

LITPLAN TEACHER PACK
for
Cheaper by the Dozen
based on the book by
Frank Gilbreth, Jr. & Ernestine Gilbreth Carey

Written by
Mary B. Collins & Barbara M. Linde

© 2006 Teacher's Pet Publications
All Rights Reserved

This **LitPlan** for *Cheaper By The Dozen*
has been brought to you by Teacher's Pet Publications, Inc.

Copyright Teacher's Pet Publications 2006

Only the student materials in this unit plan (such as worksheets,
study questions, and tests) may be reproduced multiple times
for use in the purchaser's classroom.

For any additional copyright questions,
contact Teacher's Pet Publications.

www.tpet.com

TABLE OF CONTENTS - *Cheaper By The Dozen*

Introduction	5
Unit Objectives	7
Reading Assignment Sheet	8
Unit Outline	9
Study Questions (Short Answer)	13
Quiz/Study Questions (Multiple Choice)	23
Pre-reading Vocabulary Worksheets	39
Lesson One (Introductory Lesson)	61
Nonfiction Assignment Sheet	75
Oral Reading Evaluation Form	65
Writing Assignment 1	68
Writing Assignment 2	73
Writing Assignment 3	76
Writing Evaluation Form	70
Vocabulary Review Activities	82
Extra Writing Assignments/Discussion ?s	79
Unit Review Activities	84
Unit Tests	89
Unit Resource Materials	127
Vocabulary Resource Materials	143

INTRODUCTION *Cheaper By The Dozen*

This unit has been designed to develop students' reading, writing, thinking, and language skills through exercises and activities related to *Cheaper By The Dozen* by Frank Gilbreth Jr. and Ernestine Gilbreth Carey. It includes eighteen lessons, supported by extra resource materials.

In the **introductory lesson** students write down and discuss their household rules. Following the introductory activity, students are given a transition to explain that household rules are important in every family, but in the book they are about to read, rules and order are especially important for the Gilbreth family since there are twelve children. Following the transition, students are given the materials they will be using during the unit.

The **reading assignments** are approximately twenty pages each; some are a little shorter while others are a little longer. Students have approximately 15 minutes of pre-reading work to do prior to each reading assignment. This pre-reading work involves reviewing the study questions for the assignment and doing some vocabulary work for several vocabulary words they will encounter in their reading.

The **study guide questions** are fact-based questions; students can find the answers to these questions right in the text. These questions come in two formats: short answer or multiple choice. The best use of these materials is probably to use the short answer version of the questions as study guides for students (since answers will be more complete), and to use the multiple choice version for occasional quizzes. If your school has the appropriate machinery, it might be a good idea to make transparencies of your answer keys for the overhead projector.

The **vocabulary work** is intended to enrich students' vocabularies as well as to aid in the students' understanding of the book. Prior to each reading assignment, students will complete a two-part worksheet for several vocabulary words in the upcoming reading assignment. Part I focuses on students' use of general knowledge and contextual clues by giving the sentence in which the word appears in the text. Students are then to write down what they think the words mean based on the words' usage. Part II nails down the definitions of the words by giving students dictionary definitions of the words and having students match the words to the correct definitions based on the words' contextual usage. Students should then have an understanding of the words when they meet them in the text.

After each reading assignment, students will go back and formulate answers for the study guide questions. Discussion of these questions serves as a **review** of the most important events and ideas presented in the reading assignments.

Students are assigned to do a **project** with this unit. The Gilbreth family always seemed to have some sort of a project going on–recorded language lessons, learning morse code, learning to type, etc. Students are to choose a project to complete during the unit and will share it with the whole class in a presentation at the end of the unit.

There is also a **group activity** in which students complete a motion study.

Two lessons are devoted to the **extra discussion questions/writing assignments**. These questions focus on interpretation, critical analysis and personal response, employing a variety of thinking skills and adding to the students' understanding of the novel.

After students complete the discussion questions, there is a **vocabulary review** lesson which pulls together all of the fragmented vocabulary lists for the reading assignments and gives students a review of all of the words they have studied.

There are three **writing assignments** in this unit, each with the purpose of informing, persuading, or having students express personal opinions. In the first assignment, students write to inform. They are to decide on an activity for their project, tell what it is, what they intend to do, and what they think they will gain from doing it. In the second assignment, students are asked to consider the importance of popularity (based on Mr. Gilbreth's comment about it in the book) and to write down their personal opinions about that topic. The third writing assignment is to persuade a parent, guardian, or elected official to do or agree to something the student wants.

In addition, there is a **nonfiction reading assignment**. Students are required to read a piece of nonfiction related in some way to *Cheaper By The Dozen*. After reading their nonfiction pieces, students will fill out a worksheet on which they answer questions regarding facts, interpretation, criticism, and personal opinions.

The **review lesson** pulls together all of the aspects of the unit. The teacher is given four or five choices of activities or games to use which all serve the same basic function of reviewing all of the information presented in the unit.

The **unit tests** come in two formats: short answer and multiple choice. As a convenience, two different tests for each format have been included. There is also an advanced short answer unit test which is even more challenging.

There are additional **support materials** included with this unit. The **unit resource materials** section includes suggestions for an in-class library, crossword and word search puzzles related to the novel, and extra vocabulary worksheets. There is a list of **bulletin board ideas** which gives the teacher suggestions for bulletin boards to go along with this unit. In addition, there is a list of **extra class activities** the teacher could choose from to enhance the unit or as a substitution for an exercise the teacher might feel is inappropriate for his/her class. **Answer keys** immediately follow the **reproducible student materials**. The student materials may be reproduced for use in the teacher's classroom without infringement of copyrights. No other portion of this unit may be reproduced without the written consent of Teacher's Pet Publications, Inc.

UNIT OBJECTIVES *Cheaper By The Dozen*

1. Students will consider the meaning of "education," and the roles of home and school in a person's education.

2. Students will compare and contrast views in the 1920s with current views about education, family, and child-rearing.

3. Students will practice reading orally and silently.

4. Students will answer questions to demonstrate their knowledge and understanding of the main events and characters in *Cheaper By The Dozen*.

5. Students will each complete an independent project which is educational and challenging.

6. The writing assignments are designed for several purposes:
    a. To check and increase students reading comprehension
    b. To make students think about the ideas presented in the novel
    c. To encourage logical thinking
    d. To provide the opportunity for students to practice good grammar and improve their use of the language
    e. To encourage students' creativity

7. Students will participate in group activities to improve their personal interaction skills.

8. Students will study vocabulary from the book to improve their own vocabularies.

9. Students will practice their public speaking skills.

READING ASSIGNMENTS *Cheaper By The Dozen*

Date Assigned	Chapters	Completion Date
	1 - 5	
	6 - 8	
	9 - 11	
	12 - 14	
	15 - 16	
	17 - 19	

UNIT OUTLINE *Cheaper By The Dozen*

1 Introduction Project Assignment	2 PVR Chapter 1 PV Chapter 2	3 Read Chapter 2 PV Chapters 3-5	4 Read Chapters 3-5	5 Study ?s 1-5 Writing Assignment #1
6 PVR Chapters 6-8	7 Study ?s 6-8 Motion Study Group Project	8 PV Chapters 9-11 Writing Assignment #2 Read 9-11	9 Study ?s 9-11 PVR 12-16	10 Study ?s 12-16 Library for Nonfiction Asst. PVR 17-19
11 Study ?s 17-19 Writing Assignment #3	12 Extra Discussion Questions	13 Extra Discussion Questions	14 Vocabulary Review	15 Project Reports
16 Project Reports	17 Unit Review	18 Unit Test		

P=Preview the Study Questions
V=Do the Vocabulary Worksheet
R=Read

STUDY GUIDE QUESTIONS

STUDY GUIDE QUESTIONS *Cheaper By The Dozen*

Chapters 1-5
1. Describe Dad.
2. Describe the incident that no one but Father remembered.
3. What was Dad's signal for everyone to gather?
4. Describe Dad's relationship with the car.
5. What joke did Father play on the children with the new car?
6. Why did the children always want to go for a drive?
7. What were the responsibilities of the older children?
8. Why did Father always insist on calling the roll?
9. How did the girls finally get rid of the "dusters"?
10. What would Father do when he got lost?
11. What did Father do during an "Unavoidable Delay"?
12. What joke did Bill play on Father?
13. Why didn't Father enter the Massachusetts Institute of Technology?
14. How did Father get started in the motion study business?
15. Why was the family council set up?

Chapters 6-8
1. Why did Lill paint the fence?
2. Why did Dad buy the victrolas?
3. Why did Dad bring home the typewriter (Moby Dick)?
4. What was "of general interest"?
5. What was Martha's talent?
6. What was Dad's one failure?
7. Why did Dad want his children to skip grades?
8. Why did Father go to school? What did he do there?
9. Why did Father encourage Sunday School even though he wasn't religious?
10. Who was Mrs. Mebane, and how did the townspeople pull her leg twice?
11. Who were the Mollers? Generally describe them.

Cheaper By The Dozen Study Questions Page 2

Chapters 9-11
  1. How did Mother change when she went home to the Mollers?
  2. Why did the children admire Grosie?
  3. What happened when the children finally decided to "feel at home"?
  4. How did the children change at the Mollers'?
  5. What happened to the children on the ride home from California?
  6. Why didn't Father want his children to get sick?
  7. Why did Father put red ink spots all over his face?
  8. Why did Father want to take moving pictures of Dr. Burton removing the tonsils of all of his children?
  9. What was Dr. Burton's mistake?
10. What was Coggin's mistake?
11. Why was the cottage called "The Shoe"?
12. Who were Peter and Maggie? What happened to them?
13. How did Dad teach the children Morse Code?
14. What is a Therblig?

Chapters 12-14
1. Why did Dad buy the Rena?
2. What did the children learn about their father after the mass mutiny?
3. Why couldn't the fifth baby have been named Lillian?
4. Why did everyone tease Mother about Robert's name?
5. Why was Father sad after Jane's birth?
6. Why were the babies terrified when Father took pictures?
7. Why did the children bury a coffin full of pencils?
8. What did the newsreel man do that the Gilbreths did not appreciate?

Cheaper By The Dozen Study Questions Page 3

Chapters 15-16
1. What was Mother's reaction whenever Dad resorted to corporal punishment?
2. How did Bill make Aunt Anne furious?
3. What did the children do to the psychologist?
4. Why did "over the Hill to the Poor House" upset Dad?
5. What entertainment by the children did Father like best?

Chapters 17-19
1. What did Dad think of the Jazz Age?
2. How did Anne get her parents to consent to letting the girls have their hair bobbed?
3. Describe Joe Scales.
4. Why didn't Dad go to the prom to chaperon Anne and Joe?
5. Why were Frank and Bill sent on the girls' dates?
6. Why was having Dad at the dances an advantage to Anne and Ernestine?
7. What did Dad say when Joe proposed to Anne?
8. Why were the younger children upset?
9. What did the children do to Motorcycle Mac?
10. What was wrong with Dad?
11. How did Mother change after Dad's death?

ANSWER KEY: STUDY QUESTIONS *Cheaper By The Dozen*

Chapters 1-5

1. Describe Dad.
    Dad was a tall, large man who was an efficiency expert. He ran his home like a factory and cut all wasted time from anything. Although he ran his home in a business-like way, he also loved practical jokes, had a good sense of humor, and gave a great deal of his time to his family.

2. Describe the incident that no one but Father remembered.
    Mother had gone away on a business trip and had left Father in charge. When she returned and asked how everything had gone, Father replied that everyone had been good except for one, and a spanking had put him in line. Mother replied that the disorderly child wasn't theirs; rather, he belonged to a neighbor.

3. What was Dad's signal for everyone to gather?
    Dad whistled, and all the kids were supposed to come line up.

4. Describe Dad's relationship with the car.
    Dad loved Foolish Carriage. He drove the car "fast" and recklessly, and he loved every minute of it.

5. What joke did Father play on the children with the new car?
    He took each child alone to the car and told each one to find the birdie in the engine. He waited for each child to start looking in the engine, and then he honked the horn.

6. Why did the children always want to go for a drive?
    Driving with Dad was exciting. The kids also appreciated having some time close to their parents.

7. What were the responsibilities of the older children?
    Each older child was responsible for taking care of a younger child. Their duties included getting the children ready for school, dressing them, and making sure their "duty charts" were properly filled out, among other things.

8. Why did Father always insist on calling the roll?
    He had had two experiences when he had left children behind by mistake.

9. How did the girls finally get rid of the "dusters"?
    After being mistaken for orphans while on a ride in Foolish Carriage, the girls complained to their mother (who sympathized with them). Mother took up their cause with Father, and the girls no longer had to wear their dusters.

10. What would Father do when he got lost?

    He would blame Mother or Anne for giving him the wrong directions. If things became hopeless, he would stop at a gas station, get directions, ignore the directions, and continue to be lost.

11. What did Father do during an "Unavoidable Delay"?

    He would take the time to find something to teach the children.

12. What joke did Bill play on Father?

    He imitated his mother's voice, telling Father that he was driving too fast. Father would then yell at Mother, who would reply that she had not said anything.

13. Why didn't Father enter the Massachusetts Institute of Technology?

    He didn't want to drain his widowed mother's finances or interfere with his sister's studies.

14. How did Father get started in the motion study business?

    He began as a bricklayer's helper, but kept finding ways that the bricklaying could be done better. He kept being promoted in the bricklaying company, and then he branched out to help other businesses do their work more efficiently.

15. Why was the family council set up?

    The cook and the handyman had too much work to do, so Mother and Father decided to divide the extra work among the kids. As "employers" and "employees," the parents and children decided to set up the council as a forum for making decisions and voicing grievances.

Chapters 6-8

1. Why did Lill paint the fence?

    According to the council's rules, the person who submitted the lowest bid for doing a special job was awarded that job. Lill agreed to paint the fence for much less than the other children; she wanted to earn money for some skates. Even though the bid was ridiculously low and the job was very difficult for little Lill, Dad held her to her contract. (Although, he did buy her a new pair of skates when she finished the fence.)

2. Why did Dad buy the victrolas?

    He wanted his children to learn to speak foreign languages. He bought the victrolas and language records so his children could listen and learn during their spare time.

3. Why did Dad bring home the typewriter (Moby Dick)?

    He had just invented a way for people to learn to type, and he wanted his kids to take advantage of his new system and to learn to type.

4. What was "of general interest"?
   Talking at the dinner table was only allowed if the topic was of general interest. Decisions about whether or not a topic was of general interest were made by Dad, who usually overruled any "kid talk" and allowed all of the talk about his work, which the kids often found boring.

5. What was Martha's talent?
   She learned to do mathematics quickly in her head.

6. What was Dad's one failure?
   He attempted to make a bird bath, and it crumbled.

7. Why did Dad want his children to skip grades?
   He wanted them to be challenged in school. He believed that his children learned so much at home, that keeping them in grades according to their chronological age would hold them back. His children were not the same as children with average parents, he thought.

8. Why did Father go to school? What did he do there?
   He would pop in at the kids' classrooms to talk with their teachers and check on their progress. Often he would interrupt the schedule and disobey the school rules, but the teachers didn't seem to mind. They liked Mr. Gilbreth because he was so personable.

9. Why did Father encourage Sunday School even though he wasn't religious?
   He believed that a successful man knows something about everything. He wanted his children to have a well-rounded education, so he sent them to Sunday School to learn about religion and the Bible.

10. Who was Mrs. Mebane, and how did the townspeople pull her leg twice?
    Mrs. Mebane was trying to organize a group of women who would be advocates of birth control. Two times people had sent her to see women who had large families, women who would not fit the position she was hoping to fill.

11. Who were the Mollers? Generally describe them.
    The Mollers were Mother's family; Moller was her maiden name. They were very wealthy and sugary sweet, addressing everyone as "Dear" so-and-so. The children thought that the Mollers were the "kissingest kin" in the world.

Chapters 9-11
1. How did Mother change when she went home to the Mollers?
   She became a little girl again, forgetting about her career and responsibilities, and letting her parents make all the decisions for her.

2. Why did the children admire Grosie?
    They admired her because she had power over their mother. When Grosie reprimanded Mother, Mother accepted it.

3. What happened when the children finally decided to "feel at home"?
    The children were dressed in their starchy, formal clothes for a tea party. While they were sitting in the garden waiting to be called, they decided that they had had enough of being little angels. They all hopped into the sprinkler water and got soaked.

4. How did the children change at the Mollers?
    They had become more affectionate like their Californian relatives.

5. What happened to the children on the ride home from California?
    They all caught the whooping cough.

6. Why didn't Father want his children to get sick?
    He said that a sick person dragged down the performance of the entire group.

7. Why did Father put red ink spots all over his face?
    He was playing a joke on the children, pretending to have the measles.

8. Why did Father want to take moving pictures of Dr. Burton removing the tonsils of all of his children?
    He wanted to do a motion study of a tonsillectomy. By studying the moving pictures of a number of operations, he could determine which motions were wasted and which ones were necessary.

9. What was Dr. Burton's mistake?
    He got Ernestine and Martha mixed up. Ernestine's tonsils did not need to be removed, but Martha's did. He told Martha that hers did not. When he got Ernestine on the table, he realize that he had made a mistake and that Martha's tonsils would have to be removed.

10. What was Coggin's mistake?
    He forgot to take the lens cap off of the camera, so none of the pictures came out. The whole point of the episode was lost; there could be no motion study of the tonsillectomy operation.

11. Why was the cottage called "The Shoe"?
    Father named it The Shoe because Mother reminded him of the old lady who lived in a shoe.

12. Who were Peter and Maggie? What happened to them?
    Peter and Maggie were the Gilbreths' pet canaries. They flew away. The ferry boat captain had a search for them, but the canaries were gone.

13. How did Dad teach the children Morse Code?
    He left coded messages painted on the walls. The messages were often clues to the whereabouts of nice surprises, so the children would want to take the time to decode them.

14. What is a Therblig?
    It is a unit of motion or thought, the basic unit on which Dad's business was built.

Chapters 12-14

1. Why did Dad buy the Rena?
   It was a present to the children for learning to swim. It was also a tool for teaching the children about boats, navigation, and other related things.

2. What did the children learn about their father after the mass mutiny?
   He really did not need their help to moor the boat.

3. Why couldn't the fifth baby have been named Lillian?
   He was a boy.

4. Why did everyone tease Mother about Robert's name?
   All the other children were given names of family members. There were no family members named Robert. Everyone teased Mother, saying that Robert was the name of her old beaux.

5. Why was Father sad after Jane's birth?
   He knew that there would be no more "latest models" in the Gilbreth family; there would be no more babies.

6. Why were the babies terrified when Father took pictures?
   Father always had huge flash explosions when he took pictures. The little ones weren't sure they all weren't going to be blown up.

7. Why did the children bury a coffin full of pencils?
   Dad got a job working for an automatic pencil company. Burying the old wooden pencils was a publicity stunt.

8. What did the newsreel man do that the Gilbreths did not appreciate?
   He took pictures of them while they were eating outdoors, and then he played it at a faster speed, making them look foolish.

Chapters 15-16
1. What was Mother's reaction whenever Dad resorted to corporal punishment?
   She would always object to the part of the anatomy on which the punishment would have been inflicted.

2. How did Bill make Aunt Anne furious?
   He slipped under the table and pretended to be a dog by hitting her legs and licking her hand. When she discovered that it was Bill and not a dog, she was furious.

3. What did the children do to the psychologist?
   The children did not like the kinds of questions that the psychologist was asking them, so they got together, stole the answers to the tests, and made up horrible lies to tell the psychologist so that she would tink they were all horribly maladjusted.

4. Why did "Over the Hill to the Poor House" upset Dad?
   He was convinced that he and Mother would end up just like the people in the movie.

5. What entertainment by the children did Father like best?
   He liked their performances in which they pretended to be Father and Mother.

Chapters 17-19
1. What did Dad think of the Jazz Age?
   He hated it. He didn't want his children or anyone else becoming involved with it.

2. How did Anne get her parents to consent to letting the girls have their hair bobbed?
   She bobbed her own and cried when it was criticized.

3. Describe Joe Scales.
   Joe Scales was a typical Jazz Age teen-aged boy "cheerleader." Because of his small size and orange and black striped blazer, looked like "what might happen if a pygmy married a barber pole."

4. Why didn't Dad go to the prom to chaperon Anne and Joe?
   Foolish Carriage would not start, and he refused to be seen in Joe's car.

5. Why were Frank and Bill sent on the girls' dates?
   They were to act as chaperons. Dad said that if things got out of hand, Frank or Bill could run for help.

6. Why was having Dad at the dances an advantage to Anne and Ernestine?
   They assumed he would see that the kids were good, and he would leave. As it happened, he became very popular, enhancing the status of his daughters among the crowd. He eventually decided that the kids were making a character of him, and quit chaperoning.

7. What did Dad say when Joe proposed to Anne?
   He said, "Throw him back, he's too small to keep!"

8. Why were the younger children upset?
   The older children were getting interests outside of the home and often did not take the time to play with their younger siblings.

9. What did the children do to Motorcycle Mac?
   They caught him peeping in Ernestine's window, so they surrounded the tree he was in and threatened to set it on fire.

10. What was wrong with Dad?
    He had a bad heart. He had known about his bad heart for quite some time, but his health was obviously failing.

11. How did Mother change after Dad's death?
    She stopped being afraid of things because there was nothing more to fear. She had faced the worst, the loss of Dad. She took charge of the household and carried on with Dad's work.

MULTIPLE CHOICE STUDY GUIDE/QUIZ QUESTIONS *Cheaper by the Dozen*

<u>Chapters 1-5</u>

1. What does Dad look like?
    A. He is tall and thin.
    B. He is short and heavy.
    C. He is tall and heavy.
    D. He is short and thin.

2. True or False: Dad ran his home like a factory and cut wasted time from everything.
    A. True
    B. False

3. True or False: Dad did not like jokes of any kind. He had no sense of humor.
    A. True
    B. False

4. One time while Mother was away, Dad spanked one child to put him in line. What did Mother say about this when she returned?
    A. She was glad that Dad had disciplined the child.
    B. She was angry because she never spanked the children.
    C. She said that the disorderly child was not theirs; he was a neighbor.
    D. She said that she did not want to know what happened when she was away.

5. What was Dad's signal for everyone to gather?
    A. He whistled.
    B. He played a song on the trumpet.
    C. He rang a large bell.
    D. He turned on a siren.

6. Dad played a joke on the children when he got a new car. He told each child to look under the hood and find the birdie in the engine. When the child started looking, Dad ____.
    A. started the engine
    B. turned on the windshield washers
    C. honked the horn
    D. blasted the radio

7. True or False: The children liked going for drives in the car.
    A. True
    B. False

Cheaper By The Dozen Multiple Choice Questions Chapters 1-5 Page 2

8. What did each of the older children have to do?
    A. They took turns doing the laundry.
    B. They did the grocery shopping and cooking.
    C. They cleaned the house.
    D. They each took care of one of the younger children.

9. Once Dad had left one of the children behind. What did he do after that to make sure it didn't happen again?
    A. He called the roll when they went out.
    B. He made the children hold onto a long rope.
    C. He made the children wear nametags.
    D. He only took two children out at any time.

10. On one car trip, the girls were upset because they were mistaken for orphans. What changed after this incident?
    A. The girls all got new, fashionable hairdos.
    B. The girls no longer had to wear their "dusters" when riding.
    C. Dad got a nameplate for the car with the family's last name on it.
    D. Mother made sure to tell everyone they were a family.

11. What was Dad's nickname for the car?
    A. Motion Machine
    B. Gilbreth's Jalopy
    C. Foolish Carriage
    D. Speed Demon

12. What would Dad do when he got lost?
    A. He would blame Mother or Anne for giving him the wrong directions.
    B. He would have the oldest boy look at the map.
    C. He would stop at a gas station, then follow the directions.
    D. He would tell Mother to drive.

13. What did Dad do during an "Unavoidable Delay"?
    A. He would take a nap.
    B. He would sing.
    C. He would read a book.
    D. He would teach the children something.

Cheaper By The Dozen Multiple Choice Questions Chapters 1-5 Page 3

14. When they were driving, one of the children would imitate Mother's voice and tell Dad he was driving too fast. Who did this?
    A. Anne
    B. Ernestine
    C. Bill
    D. Frank

15. Why didn't Dad enter the Massachusetts Institute of Technology?
    A. He was not smart enough to get accepted.
    B. He did not think the school was good enough for him.
    C. He did not want to drain his mother's finances.
    D. His parents would not let him go that far away from home.

16. What field of work was Dad in?
    A. motion study
    B. architect
    C. medicine
    D. farmer

17. How did the family make decisions and voice grievances?
    A. The parents made all decisions and did not listen to complaints.
    B. They set up a Family Council.
    C. The younger children told the older ones and they spoke with the parents.
    D. Everyone did what they wanted to do.

Cheaper By The Dozen Multiple Choice Questions Chapters 6-8

1. Which statement about the fence painting is true?
    A. Dad hired a professional painter and took the cost out of the children's' allowances.
    B. All of the children painted for free.
    C. Lil got the job because she was the lowest bidder.
    D. Mother painted it because she liked working outside.

2. What did Dad do to help the children learn foreign languages?
    A. He hired tutors who spoke French, Spanish, and German.
    B. He took the family to other countries.
    C. He read them books in other languages.
    D. He bought victrolas and language records.

3. Dad had invented a new system and wanted the children to try it out. What kind of machine did he bring home to do this?
    A. typewriter
    B. computer
    C. calculator
    D. washing machine

4. Talking at the dinner table was allowed only if the topic was of general interest. What did Dad consider to be general interest?
    A. politics
    B. current events
    C. family happenings
    D. his work

5. What was Martha's talent?
    A. juggling
    B. doing math quickly in her head
    C. singing
    D. fixing broken appliances

6. What was Dad's one failure?
    A. He tried to make a birdbath, but it crumpled.
    B. He tried to make an oven that turned itself on, but it didn't work.
    C. He tried to make a speaker system in the house but he could not do the wiring.
    D. He tried to sew a dress for Mother but it came out the wrong size.

Cheaper By The Dozen Multiple Choice Questions Chapters 6-8 Page 2

7. Dad thought his children were not the same as children with average parents. What did he do to promote this idea?
    A. He started his own school for his children.
    B. He pushed for his children to skip grades at the public school.
    C. He gave the children extra assignments at home.
    D. He sent them to an exclusive private prep school.

8. Father would often check on the children's progress at school. How did the teachers respond to him coming in and interrupting their classes?
    A. They didn't mind because they liked him.
    B. They locked their doors and told him to stay out.
    C. They put him to work.
    D. They threatened to fail the children if he didn't stop coming in.

9. Father wanted his children to have a well-rounded education so he __.
    A. had them work at a homeless shelter
    B. sent them to Sunday School
    C. made them all get part-time jobs
    D. had them join the Girl or Boy Scouts

10. Mrs. Mebane came to the town to organize a group of women who would be advocates of _____.
    A. birth control
    B. the right to vote for women
    C. equal pay for equal work
    D. admitting women to male-only colleges

11. True or False: The townspeople pulled Mrs. Mebane's leg by twice sending her to see women who had large families.
    A. True
    B. False

12. Who were the Mollers?
    A. They were the hired couple who did the gardening and cooking.
    B. They were Dad's family.
    C. They were Mom's family.
    D. They were Dad's business partners.

Cheaper By The Dozen Multiple Choice Questions Chapters 6-8 Page 3

13. How did the Mollers address everyone?
    A. "Sweetheart"
    B. "Hey, you"
    C. "Kiddo"
    D. "Dear"

14. Which sentence best describes the Mollers?
    A. very wealthy and sugary sweet
    B. hard working but poor
    C. uneducated and ill-mannered
    D. middle class and very intelligent

Cheaper By The Dozen Multiple Choice Questions Chapters 9-11

1. True or False: When Mother went home to her parents and family, she became like a little girl again.
    A. True
    B. False

2. Why did the children admire Grosie?
    A. She could do magic tricks.
    B. She had power over their mother.
    C. She spoke twelve languages.
    D. She gave them many presents.

3. What happened when the children finally decided to "feel at home"?
    A. They wrote on the bedroom walls with crayons.
    B. They put toilet paper all over the outside of the house.
    C. They hopped into the garden sprinklers and got wet.
    D. They all refused to eat dinner at the same time.

4. True or False: During the time at the Mollers, the children became cold and unfeeling.
    A. True
    B. False

5. On the ride home from California, the children caught ___.
    A. whooping cough
    B. measles
    C. mumps
    D. chicken pox

6. What did Dad say about sickness?
    A. It was a natural part of life.
    B. It gave a person time to rest and think.
    C. It was preventable with a proper life style.
    D. It dragged down the performance of the entire group.

7. True or False: Dad put red spots on his face, pretending he had the measles.
    A. True
    B. False

8. What event did Dad want to film and study?
    A. the children's tonsillectomies
    B. one of Mother's speeches
    C. the birth of the last of the children
    D. his own sleep habits

Cheaper By The Dozen Multiple Choice Questions Chapters 9-11 Page 2

9. Which of the two children did Dr. Burton mix up?
 A. Dan and Jack
 B. Ernestine and Martha
 C. Bill and Fred
 D. Ann and Lil

10. What was Coggin's mistake?
 A. He forgot to get permission for the filming, so it could not be done.
 B. He forgot to take the lens cap off the camera so none of the pictures came out.
 C. He forgot to close the back of the camera and ruined the film.
 D. He slept late and arrived too late to do the filming.

11. What did Dad call the cottage?
 A. The Big House in the Woods
 B. Camp Gilbreth
 C. The Castle of Fun
 D. The Shoe

12. What happened to Peter and Maggie?
 A. They flew away.
 B. They bought a house next to the Gilbreth family.
 C. They were eaten by the Gilbreth's dog.
 D. They bought part of Dad's business.

13. What did Dad teach by leaving messages on the walls? The messages were clues to the whereabouts of nice surprises.
 A. Spanish
 B. Latin
 C. Morse Code
 D. shorthand

14. A ____ is a unit of motion or thought, the basic unit on which Dad's business was built.
 A. Kimchee
 B. Therblig
 C. Quark
 D. Nanosecond

Cheaper By The Dozen Multiple Choice Questions Chapters 12-14

1. Why did Dad buy the Rena?
    A. It was a present to the children for learning to swim.
    B. It was an anniversary gift for Mother.
    C. It was meant to be used to entertain his business clients.
    D. He wanted a place to get away from the noise of the family.

2. What did the children learn about their father after the mass mutiny?
    A. He really did need their help to moor the boat.
    B. He really did not need their help to moor the boat.
    (Two choices only.)

3. True or False: The fifth baby was a girl named Lillian.
    A. True
    B. False

4. Everyone said that Mother named the baby after _____.
    A. her favorite movie star
    B. her favorite book character
    C. an old boyfriend
    D. her editor

5. True or False: Dad knew that Jane would be the last baby.
    A. True
    B. False

6. The _____ terrified the babies when Dad took pictures.
    A. huge flash explosions
    B. size of the camera
    C. sound of the shutter clicking
    D. need to sit perfectly still

7. What stunt did the children do when Dad got a job with an automatic pencil company?
    A. They all learned to write with their toes.
    B. They built a ten-foot tall pencil out of pencils.
    C. They gave out pencils to everyone in the school.
    D. They buried old wooden pencils in a coffin.

Cheaper By The Dozen Multiple Choice Questions Chapters 12-14 Page 2

8. What did the newsreel man do that the Gilbreths did not appreciate?
    A. He took pictures of them eating and played them faster to make the family look foolish.
    B. He took pictures that Dad had told him not to take.
    C. He sold the pictures to a television station and kept the money.
    D. He destroyed the film before making a copy for them.

Cheaper By The Dozen Multiple Choice Questions Chapters 15-16

Chapters 15-16
1. What was Mother's response whenever Dad resorted to corporal punishment?
     A. She went to her room and locked the door.
     B. She gave the child a pillow for protection.
     C. She objected to the part of the anatomy which was being hit.
     D. She cried until Dad stopped.

2. How did Bill make Aunt Anne furious?
     A. He short-sheeted her bed.
     B. He crawled under the table and acted like a dog, licking her hand.
     C. He put salt in the sugar bowl.
     D. He put bleach in a load of her laundry and ruined her clothes.

3. True or False: The children made up lies so the psychologist would think they are maladjusted.
     A. True
     B. False

4. What was the name of the movie that upset Dad, because he was sure the family would end up like the people in the movie?
     A. "Over the Hill to the Poor House"
     B. "Six Days to Disaster"
     C. "A Tale of Failure"
     D. "Old and Alone"

5. What entertainment by the children did Dad like best?
     A. He liked to hear them sing.
     B. He liked to watch them put on Shakespeare plays.
     C. He liked it when they pretended to be Dad and Mother.
     D. He liked it when they danced and did magic tricks.

Cheaper By The Dozen Multiple Choice Questions Chapters 17-19

Chapters 17-19

1. What did Dad think of the Jazz Age?
    A. He liked it.
    B. He hated it.
    C. He did not care about it.
    D. He said he could get used to it.

2. Anne did something that her parents did not want her to. She cried when she was criticized. Her behavior resulted in getting her parents' consent for the girls to ____.
    A. wear nylon stockings get
    B. start to date
    C. get their hair bobbed
    D. get a telephone in their bedroom

3. Which sentence describes Joe Scales?
    A. "What might happen if a gorilla married a swan."
    B. "What might happen if a pygmy married a barber pole."
    C. "What might happen if a car salesman married a supermodel."
    D. "What might happen if a genius married a worm."

4. Why didn't Dad go to the prom to chaperone Anne and Joe?
    A. He wanted to give them their privacy.
    B. He was busy with business dealings.
    C. He did not want to wear a tuxedo.
    D. Foolish Carriage would not start and he refused to be seen in Joe's car.

5. Who went with the girls on dates?
    A. Tom
    B. Dad
    C. Frank and Bill
    D. Bob and Jack

6. How did Dad die?
    A. He was hit by a car.
    B. The ship he was on sunk.
    C. He had a heart attack.
    D. He caught pneumonia.

Cheaper By The Dozen Multiple Choice Questions Chapters 17-19 Page 2

7. What did Mother do after Dad died?
    A. She moved the family to California to live with her parents.
    B. She went on with Dad's work.
    C. She went back to college.
    D. She became depressed and stayed in bed for six months.

ANSWER KEY - MULTIPLE CHOICE STUDY/QUIZ QUESTIONS
Cheaper by the Dozen

Ch. 1-5	Ch. 6-8	Ch. 9-11	Ch. 12-14	Ch. 15-16	Ch. 17-19
1. C	1. C	1. A	1. A	1. C	1. B
2. A	2. D	2. B	2. B	2. B	2. C
3. B	3. A	3. C	3. B	3. A	3. B
4. C	4. D	4. B	4. C	4. A	4. D
5. A	5. B	5. A	5. A	5. C	5. C
6. C	6. A	6. D	6. A		6. C
7. A	7. B	7. A	7. D		7. B
8. D	8. A	8. A	8. A		
9. A	9. B	9. B			
10. B	10. A	10. B			
11. C	11. A	11. D			
12. A	12. C	12. A			
13. D	13. D	13. C			
14. C	14. A	14. B			
15. C					
16. A					
17. B					

VOCABULARY WORKSHEETS

VOCABULARY CHAPTER 1 *Cheaper By The Dozen*

Part I: Using Prior Knowledge and Contextual Clues

Below are the sentences in which the vocabulary words appear in the text. Read the sentence. Use any clues you can find in the sentence combined with your prior knowledge, and write what you think the underlined words mean on the lines provided.

1. He was no longer slim; he had passed the two-hundred-pound mark during his early thirties, and left it so far behind that there were times when he had to resort to railway baggage scales to <u>ascertain</u> his displacement.

   _____

2. But he carried himself with the self-assurance of a successful gentleman who was proud of his wife, proud of his family, and proud of his business accomplishments. Dad had enough <u>gall</u> to be divided into three parts.

   _____

3, 4. But bear in mind the trouble most parents have in getting just one child off to school, and multiply it by twelve. Some <u>regimentation</u> was necessary to prevent <u>bedlam</u>.

   _____

   _____

5. Although he was a strict taskmaster within his home, Dad <u>tolerated</u> no criticism of the family from outsiders.

   _____

6. . . . one reason he had wanted a large family was to assure himself of an <u>appreciative</u> audience, even within the confines of his home. With us around, he could always be sure of a full house, packed tot he galleries.

   _____

7. The call was important. It meant drop everything and come running–or risk <u>dire</u> consequences.

   _____

8. At the first note, Gilbreth children came dashing from all corners of the house and yard. Neighborhood dogs, barking hellishly, <u>converged</u> for blocks around.

   _____

Cheaper By The Dozen Vocabulary Worksheet Chapter 1 Continued

9. "What's going on?"
"The Gilbreths' house is on fire," he replied, "thank God!"
"Shall I call the fire department?" she shouted?
"What's the matter, are you crazy?" the husband answered <u>incredulously</u>.

Part II: Determining the Meaning -- Match the vocabulary words to their dictionary definitions.

___ 1. Ascertain   A. Expressing disbelief
___ 2. Gall   B. Noisy uproar and confusion
___ 3. Regimentation   C. To find out
___ 4. Bedlam   D. Terrible; disastrous
___ 5. Tolerate   E. Feeling or showing gratitude or pleasure
___ 6. Appreciative   F. Approached the same point from different directions
___ 7. Dire   G. Self-assertiveness
___ 8. Converged   H. Uniformity and discipline
___ 9. Incredulously   I. To allow without opposing

VOCABULARY CHAPTER 2 *Cheaper By The Dozen*

Part I: Using Prior Knowledge and Contextual Clues

Below are the sentences in which the vocabulary words appear in the text. Read the sentence. Use any clues you can find in the sentence combined with your prior knowledge, and write what you think the underlined words mean on the lines provided.

1. Although Dad made his living by redesigning complicated machinery, so as to reduce the number of human motions required to operate it, he never really understood the mechanical intricacies of our automobile.

_____

2. Dad had seen the car in the factory and fallen in love with it. The affection was entirely one-sided and unrequited.

_____

3. The contraption kicked him when he cranked, spit oil in his face when he looked into its bowels, squealed when he mashed the brakes, and rumbled ominously when he shifted gears.

_____

4. But he did drive it fast. He terrified all of us, but particularly Mother. She sat next to him on the front seat–with two of the babies on her lap–and alternated between clutching Dad's arm and closing her eyes in supplication.

_____

5. The lookout on the front seat was Dad's own idea. The other safety measures, which we soon inaugurated as a matter of self-preservation, were our own.

_____

6. Dad jumped so high he actually toppled into the engine leaving his feet dangling in mid-air. Finally he managed to extricate himself.

_____

Part II: Determining the Meaning -- Match the vocabulary words to their dictionary definitions.

____ 1. Intricacies   A. Not returned
____ 2. Unrequited   B. Began
____ 3. Ominously   C. Many complexly arranged elements
____ 4. Supplication   D. Release from entanglement
____ 5. Inaugurated   E. Prayer; humble begging
____ 6. Extricate   F. Threateningly

VOCABULARY CHAPTER 3 *Cheaper By The Dozen*

Part I: Using Prior Knowledge and Contextual Clues

Below are the sentences in which the vocabulary words appear in the text. Read the sentence. Use any clues you can find in the sentence combined with your prior knowledge, and write what you think the underlined words mean on the lines provided.

1. "How many want to go for a ride?" The question was purley <u>rhetorical</u>, for when Dad rode, everybody rode.

___

2, 3. Although Dad's driving was <u>fraught</u> with <u>peril</u>, there was a strange fascination n its brushes with death and its dramatic, traffic-stopping scenes.

___

___

4, 5. Dad was a <u>perpetual</u> <u>optimist;</u> confident that brains someday would triumph over inanimate steel. . . .

___

___

6. The other occurrence was slightly more <u>lurid</u>. We were en route from Montclair to New Bedford, Massachusetts, and Frank, Jr. Was left behind by mistake in a restaurant in New London. His absence wasn't discovered until near the end of the trip.

___

7. Finally, off we'd start. Mother, holding the two babies, seemed to glow with <u>vitality</u>.

___

8. He'd slow down to five miles an hour and he'd blow the horns at imaginary obstacles and cars two blocks away. The horns were Dad's <u>calliope</u>.

___

9. Whenever the crowds gathered at some intersection where we were stopped by traffic, the <u>inevitable</u> question came sooner or later.

___

10. Dad was all set to go into a new act–the <u>benevolent</u> superintendent taking the little orphan tykes out for a drive.

___

Cheaper By The Dozen Vocabulary Chapter 3 Continued

11. "That," she said, "is the last straw. Positively and emphatically the <u>ultimate</u> straw."

___

12, 13. That's the funniest thing I ever heard in my life. An orphanage on wheels. And me the superintendent. Gilbreth's Retreat for the Red-Haired Offspring of Unwed but <u>Repentant Reprobates</u>.

___

___

Part II: Determining the Meaning -- Match the vocabulary words to their dictionary definitions.

___ 1. Rhetorical   A. Final; best or most extreme example of its kind
___ 2. Fraught   B. Lasting forever
___ 3. Peril   C. Energy
___ 4. Perpetual   D. Only one or no answer is expected
___ 5. Optimist   E. Filled with (usually something undesirable)
___ 6. Lurid   F. a musical keyboard fitted with steam whistles
___ 7. Vitality   G. Morally unprincipled people
___ 8. Calliope   H. Unavoidable; going to happen no matter what
___ 9. Inevitable   I. feeling sorry for a wrong doing
___10. Benevolent   J. Danger
___11. Ultimate   K. Causing shock or horror
___12. Reprobates   L. One who always expects a favorable outcome
___13. Repentant   M. Kind; charitable

VOCABULARY CHAPTERS 4-5 *Cheaper By The Dozen*

Part I: Using Prior Knowledge and Contextual Clues

Below are the sentences in which the vocabulary words appear in the text. Read the sentence. Use any clues you can find in the sentence combined with your prior knowledge, and write what you think the underlined words mean on the lines provided.

1. When he ate an apple, he consumed skin, core, and seeds, which he alleged were the most healthful and most <u>delectable</u> portions of the fruit.

2. Neither Dad nor Mother thought filling station toilets were sanitary. They never elaborated about just what diseases the toilets contained, but they made it plain that the ailments were both <u>contagious</u> and dire.

3. Dad always opened the door of a public rest room with his coattail, and the preparations and precautions that <u>ensued</u> were "unavoidable delay" in its worst aspect.

4, 5. "You're the one who came here to learn," the foreman hollered at him. "For Christ's sake don't try to learn us." <u>Subtle</u> <u>innuendoes</u> like that never worried Dad.

6. "Your chairman recognizes the assistant chairman," he said, nodding to Mother to let her know he had just <u>conferred</u> that title upon her person.

7. When it came to apportioning work on an <u>aptitude</u> basis, the smaller girls were assigned to dust the legs and lower shelves of furniture; the older girls to dust table tops and upper shelves. The older boys would push the lawn mowers and carry leaves. The younger ones would do the raking and weeding.

8. Martha, who had been carefully coached in private <u>caucus</u>, arose.

9. "So many as favor the motion to spend only ninety-five-dollars, signify by saying aye." The motion carried <u>unanimously</u>.

10. He looked pleadingly at Mother. "Lillie, Lillie, open your eyes," he <u>implored</u>. Don't you see where this is leading us? . . ."

Cheaper By The Dozen Vocabulary Chapters 4-5 Continued

Part II: Determining the Meaning -- Match the vocabulary words to their dictionary definitions.

___ 1. Delectable   A. Not immediately obvious
___ 2. Contagious   B. A meeting to decide upon questions of policy
___ 3. Ensue   C. Bestowed or given as an honor
___ 4. Subtle   D. Enjoyable; delightful
___ 5. Innuendoes   E. In complete agreement
___ 6. Conferred   F. Tending to spread from one to another
___ 7. Aptitude   G. To follow immediately after
___ 8. Caucus   H. Things (usually negative) implied or suggested
___ 9. Unanimously   I. Begged for urgently
___10. Implored   J. Ability

VOCABULARY CHAPTERS 6-8 *Cheaper By The Dozen*

Part I: Using Prior Knowledge and Contextual Clues

Below are the sentences in which the vocabulary words appear in the text. Read the sentence. Use any clues you can find in the sentence combined with your prior knowledge, and write what you think the underlined words mean on the lines provided.

1. Like most of Dad's and Mother's ideas, the Family Council was basically sound and, although it verged sometimes on the hysterical, brought results.

2. But your French accents are so atrocious that no one but yourselves could possibly understand you.

3. Dad entered Ernestine's name in a national speed contest, as a sort of child prodigy, but Mother talked him out of it and Ern never actually competed.

4. I know you didn't touch it, and I'm sorry I implied that you did.

5. The standard reward for skipping was a new bicycle. . . . the bicycle incentive was great. . . .

6. When we moved to Montclair, the business of enrolling us in the public schools was first on the agenda.

7. And a stewardess told me that her behind had been pinched surreptitiously so many times between Hoboken and Liverpool that she had to eat off a mantelpiece.

8. "How perfectly frightful. She impressed me as quite normal. Not at all like an eight-child woman." "She's kept her youth well," Mother conceded.

9. "We'd like you to be the moving spirit behind a Montclair birth control chapter." Mother decided at this point that the situation was too ludicrous for Dad to miss, and that he'd never forgive her if she didn't deal him in.

Cheaper By The Dozen Vocabulary Chapters 6-8 Continued

10. As Dad and Mother, dressed in dusters and wearing goggles, went scorching through the streets of Boston, bystanders tossed insults and <u>ridicule</u> in their direction.

11. "Say, Noah, what are you doing with that Ark?"
That did it. Dad slowed the car and cocked his checkered cap <u>belligerently</u> over one eye. "Collecting animals like the good Lord told me," he screamed back. "All I need now is a jackass. Hop in."

12. Certainly rigid attention wasn't the most efficient way to drive an automobile. Anyone with half an eye could see the posture was <u>fatiguing</u> to the point of exhaustion.

Part II: Determining the Meaning -- Match the vocabulary words to their dictionary definitions.

____ 1. Verged   A. Aggressive; hostile
____ 2. Atrocious   B. Tiring
____ 3. Prodigy   C. List of things to be done
____ 4. Implied   D. Make fun of
____ 5. Incentive   E. A reward offered to motivate one to action
____ 6. Agenda   F. Admitted; acknowledged as true
____ 7. Surreptitious   G. Laughable because it's ridiculous or foolish
____ 8. Conceded   H. Person with exceptional talents
____ 9. Ludicrous   I. Bordered; edged
____10. Ridicule   J. Exceptionally bad
____11. Belligerent   K. Performed or acquired by secret means
____12. Fatiguing   L. Indicated by suggestion rather than directly

VOCABULARY CHAPTER 9 *Cheaper By The Dozen*

Part I: Using Prior Knowledge and Contextual Clues

Below are the sentences in which the vocabulary words appear in the text. Read the sentence. Use any clues you can find in the sentence combined with your prior knowledge, and write what you think the underlined words mean on the lines provided.

1. But the biggest change was in Mother. <u>Ensconced</u> again in the bedroom in which she had grown up, she seemed to shed her responsibilities and become again "one of the Moller girls."

___

2. Since Mother seemed so concerned about Grosie and Papa, we held them in <u>awe</u>. We tiptoed in their presence and talked only in whispers.

___

3. The respect in which we held Grosie was heightened the day after our arrival, when she gave Mother a quick <u>reprimand</u> which Mother accepted just as if she were a little girl again.

___

4, 5. To be efficient, in the Gilbreth family, was a virtue on par with <u>veracity</u>, honesty, generosity, <u>philanthropy</u>, and tooth-brushing.

___

___

6. Bill finally was prevailed upon to dress in his new outfit. But he was <u>sullen</u>, and so were the rest of us when we received our instructions about the party.

___

7. Frank and Bill joined Martha under the sprinkler. Then Ernestine came in, thus leaving Anne, the oldest, in what for her was a fairly familiar <u>dilemma</u>, whether to cast her lot with us or with the adults.

___

8. It was <u>tacitly</u> understood in the Moller family that the less one knew about his cooking methods and what he put into the food, the better for all concerned.

___

9. Dad had managed to <u>obtain</u> leave from Fort Sill, and surprised us by boarding the train at Chicago.

___

Cheaper By The Dozen Vocabulary Chapter 9 Continued

Part II: Determining the Meaning -- Match the vocabulary words to their dictionary definitions.

____ 1. Ensconced   A. Truthfulness
____ 2. Awe   B. Get; acquire
____ 3. Reprimand   C. Showing ill-humor or resentment
____ 4. Veracity   D. An emotion of respect and wonder tinged with fear
____ 5. Philanthropy   E. Not spoken; implied or inferred
____ 6. Sullen   F. A scolding, punishment or correction for doing something wrong
____ 7. Dilemma   G. Settled securely
____ 8. Tacitly   H. A situation requiring a choice
____ 9. Obtain   I. Giving charitable donations or aid

VOCABULARY CHAPTERS 10-11 *Cheaper By The Dozen*

Part I: Using Prior Knowledge and Contextual Clues

Below are the sentences in which the vocabulary words appear in the text. Read the sentence. Use any clues you can find in the sentence combined with your prior knowledge, and write what you think the underlined words mean on the lines provided.

1. "A child abed mends best if left to himself," Grandma said, while Dad nodded approval. Mother said she agreed, too, but then she proceeded to wait on the sick child hand and foot. "Here, darling, put my lovely bed jacket around your shoulders," Mother would tell the <u>ailing</u> one.

2. A cousin brought measles into the house, and all of us except Martha were stricken <u>simultaneously</u>. Two big adjoining bedrooms upstairs were converted into hospital wards....

3. It was shortly after the measles epidemic that Dad started applying motion study to surgery to try to reduce the time required for certain operations. "<u>Surgeons</u> aren't much different from skilled mechanics," Dad said, "except that they're not so skilled."

4. The first day that we children were well enough to get up, Dad and Mother set out in the car for Dr. Burton's office. Mother had urged Dad to call a taxi. She didn't know how to drive, and she said Dad probably wouldn't feel like doing the driving on the way home. But Dad laughed at her <u>qualms</u>.

5. The cottage and lighthouses were situated on a flat stretch of land between the fashionable Cliff and the Bathing Beach. Besides our place, there was only one other house in the <u>vicinity</u>. This belonged to an artist couple named Whitney.

6. Fred nodded. Dad pointed to the empty cage. "Two canaries," Dad shouted, "known as Peter and Maggie and by other <u>aliases</u> have flown the coop. No matter.

7. He'd swim under water a ways, allow his feet to <u>emerge</u>, wiggle his toes, swim under water some more, then come up head first....

8. A lazy man, Dad believed, always makes the best use of his Therbligs because he is too <u>indolent</u> to waste motions. Whenever Dad started to do a new motion study project at a factory, he'd always begin by announcing he wanted to photograph the motions of the laziest man on the job.

Cheaper By The Dozen Vocabulary Chapters 10-11 Continued

9. Meanwhile, *The Shoe* and the lighthouses had become a stop on some of the Nantucket sightseeing tours. The stop didn't <u>entail</u> getting out of the carriages or, later, the buses

_____

10. Mother was <u>irked</u>. "I never heard of such a thing in all my born days. Imagine taking perfect strangers through our bedrooms, and the house a wreck, most likely."

_____

Part II: Determining the Meaning -- Match the vocabulary words to their dictionary definitions.

___ 1. Ailing	A.	Issues causing uneasiness
___ 2. Simultaneous	B.	Irritated; annoyed
___ 3. Surgeons	C.	Ill
___ 4. Qualms	D.	Lazy
___ 5. Vicinity	E.	To have a necessary accompaniment or consequences
___ 6. Alias	F.	Doctors who perform operations
___ 7. Emerge	G.	At the same time
___ 8. Indolent	H.	An assumed name
___ 9. Entail	I.	Neighborhood; area
___ 10. Irked	J.	To come forth from; come into sight

VOCABULARY CHAPTERS 12-16 *Cheaper By The Dozen*

Part I: Using Prior Knowledge and Contextual Clues
   Below are the sentences in which the vocabulary words appear in the text. Read the sentence. Use any clues you can find in the sentence combined with your prior knowledge, and write what you think the underlined words mean on the lines provided.

1. Dad acquired the *Rena* to reward us for learning to swim. She was a catboat, twenty feet long and almost as wide. She was <u>docile</u>, dignified, and ancient.

   _____

2. Dad was never happier than when aboard the *Rena*. From the moment he climbed into our <u>dory</u> to row out to *Rena*'s mooring, his personality changed.

   _____

3. "Avast there, you swabs," Dad hollered. "No <u>mutinous</u> whispering on the poop deck!"

   _____

4, 5. Dad's mood was contagious, and soon the mates were as dogmatic and as full of <u>invective</u> as he, when dealing with the sneaking pickpockets and rum-palsied <u>derelicts</u> who were their subordinates.

   _____

   _____

6. It was a year or so after the wedding, when Mother was expecting her first baby, that Dad confided to her his secret <u>conviction</u> that all of their children would be girls.

   _____

7. He always forbade baby talk in the presence of Anne or any of his <u>subsequent</u> offspring.

   _____

8. Dad and Mother timed their books to <u>coincide</u> with Mother's annual intervals of unavoidable delay.

   _____

9. Having fathered one son, Dad took it pretty much for granted that all the rest of his children would be boys. "The first four were just practice," he'd say to Mother, while glaring with assumed <u>ferocity</u> at the girls. "Of course, I suppose we ought to keep them."

   _____

10. When Mr. Coggin departed after the unfortunate <u>debacle</u> concerning our tonsils, a series of other professional cameramen came and went.

   _____

Cheaper By The Dozen Vocabulary Chapters 12-16 Continued

11. But at least they had adopted a <u>fatalistic</u> attitude that death, if it came, would be swift and painless.

12. "There sat Mrs. Gilbreth, surrounded by her brood, reading aloud a fairy tale," Dad would read. "The oldest, almost <u>debutante</u> Anne, wants to be a professional violinist. Ernestine intends to be a painter, Martha and Frank to follow in their father's footsteps.

13. And I hate and <u>detest</u> people who make depreciating moues. I never made one in my life, or at any rate not since I've been old enough to know better.

14. Even when Dad administered vitally needed punishment on the conventional area, the area where it is supposed to do the most good, Mother tried to <u>intervene</u>.

15. We hated her and suspected that the feeling was <u>mutual</u>.

16. Then we pretended to walk up a flight of stairs, to <u>indicate</u> that we had entered the factory.

17. "That thing a drill press?" Fred said with an exaggerated lisp. "Haw."
"<u>Precisely</u>," said Frank. " Explain it to him, in simple language."

Cheaper By The Dozen Vocabulary Chapters 12-16 Continued

Part II: Determining the Meaning -- Match the vocabulary words to their dictionary definitions.

____ 1. Docile	A.	Young woman who is formally presented to society
____ 2. Dory	B.	Exactly
____ 3. Mutinous	C.	Small, narrow, flat-bottomed boat
____ 4. Invective	D.	Belief that events are predetermined; submission to fate
____ 5. Derelicts	E.	Possessed in common
____ 6. Subsequent	F.	Dislike intensely
____ 7. Conviction	G.	Demonstrate or point out
____ 8. Coincide	H.	Obedient; submissive to management
____ 9. Ferocity	I.	Strong belief
____10. Debacle	J.	Rebellious
____11. Fatalistic	K.	To come between; interfere
____12. Debutante	L.	Social outcasts
____13. Detest	M.	Savage fierceness
____14. Intervene	N.	Following in order
____15. Mutual	O.	Insults
____16. Indicate	P.	Disaster
____17. Precisely	Q.	To happen at the same time

VOCABULARY CHAPTERS 17-19 *Cheaper By The Dozen*

Part I: Using Prior Knowledge and Contextual Clues

Below are the sentences in which the vocabulary words appear in the text. Read the sentence. Use any clues you can find in the sentence combined with your prior knowledge, and write what you think the underlined words mean on the lines provided.

1. By the time Anne was a senior in high school, Dad was convinced that the current generation of girls was riding, with rouged lips and rolled stockings, straight for a jazzy and probably illicit <u>rendezvous</u> with the greasy-haired devil.

___

2. Silk stockings indeed! I don't want to hear another word out of either of you, or into the <u>convent</u> you go.

___

3. "No, sir," the girls shouted <u>indignantly</u>. "You don't touch a hair on her head. The idea "

___

4. Having <u>capitulated</u> on the hair question, Dad put up an even sterner resistance against any future changes in dress.

___

5. Clothes remained a subject of considerable friction, but the matter that threatened to affect Dad's stability was jazz. Radios were <u>innocuous</u>, being still in the catwhisker and headphone stage, and featuring such stimulating programs as the Arling Time Signals. But five- and six-piece dance bands were turning out huge piles of graphophone records, and we tried to buy them all.

___

6. The exhaust whistle, coupled with the natural engine noises, <u>precluded</u> the necessity of Mister Scales' giving any further notice about the car's arrival at its destination.

___

7. When Dad couldn't act as a chaperone himself, he sent Frank or Bill along as his <u>proxy</u>.

___

8. "Well, nobody asked you," Mother said, "so perhaps you'd better <u>forgo</u> any further speculation.

___

Cheaper By The Dozen Vocabulary Chapters 17-19 Continued

9, 10. "The first thing I know you'll be greasing your hair and wearing one of those yellow slickers," Mother <u>admonished</u> him with <u>mock</u> severity.

_____

_____

11. Anne, Ernestine, and Martha had less and less time for family games, for plays and skits. It was the inevitable <u>prelude</u> to growing up.

_____

Part II: Determining the Meaning -- Match the vocabulary words to their dictionary definitions.

____ 1. Rendezvous   A. Give up
____ 2. Convent   B. Imitation; false
____ 3. Indignantly   C. Harmless
____ 4. Capitulated   D. Home for nuns
____ 5. Innocuous   E. Prearranged meeting
____ 6. Precluded   F. Event or action preceding a more important one
____ 7. Proxy   G. Yielded; gave in
____ 8. Forgo   H. Kindly but seriously reprimanded
____ 9. Admonished   I. Prevented; made impossible by a previous action
____10. Mock   J. Person authorized to act for another
____11. Prelude   K. Angrily because of something unjust

ANSWER KEY - VOCABULARY
Cheaper By The Dozen

	1	2	3	4-5	6-8	9	10-11	12-16	17-19
1	C	C	D	D	I	G	C	H	E
2	G	A	E	F	J	D	G	C	D
3	H	F	J	G	H	F	F	J	K
4	B	E	B	A	L	A	A	O	G
5	I	B	L	H	E	I	I	L	C
6	E	D	K	C	C	C	H	N	I
7	D		C	J	K	H	J	I	J
8	F		F	B	F	E	D	Q	A
9	A		H	E	G	B	E	M	H
10			M	I	D		B	P	B
11			A		A			D	F
12			G		B			A	
13			I					F	
14								K	
15								E	
16								G	
17								B	

DAILY LESSONS

LESSON ONE

Objectives
1. To introduce *Cheaper By The Dozen* unit
2. To distribute books, study guides and other related materials

NOTE: Prior to this lesson, prepare a bulletin board with background paper and title it: HOUSEHOLD RULES.

Activity #1
Tell students to take out a piece of paper and to make a list of all of the rules in their households. Give students about 5 minutes to jot down their lists. Have students tell some of their household rules to the class, and jot them down on the bulletin board. (You might want to have drawn guide lines on the board if you have trouble writing straight.) Have students discuss the reasons why these various rules are necessary.

Transition: Tell students that the book they are going to read is about a family with twelve children, and that those children have many rules to follow just to keep the household from being chaotic! Sometimes, though, even with rules, things get a bit out of hand resulting in hilarious episodes! These kids have a father who is a "motion study man," an expert in efficiency, who is constantly finding a better way to do things and inventing unusual projects for his kids to complete.

Activity #2
Distribute the Project Assignment Sheet and discuss the directions in detail. Be sure to tell students if there will be a time limit on their presentations.

Activity #3
Distribute the materials students will use in this unit. Explain in detail how students are to use these materials.

Study Guides Students should preview the study guide questions before each reading assignment to get a feeling for what events and ideas are important in that section. After reading the section, students will (as a class or individually) answer the questions to review the important events and ideas from that section of the book. Students should keep the study guides as study materials for the unit test.

Vocabulary Prior to reading a reading assignment, students will do vocabulary work related to the section of the book they are about to read. Following the completion of the reading of the book, there will be a vocabulary review of all the words used in the vocabulary assignments. Students should keep their vocabulary work as study materials for the unit test.

Reading Assignment Sheet   You need to fill in the reading assignment sheet to let students know when their reading has to be completed. You can either write the assignment sheet on a side blackboard or bulletin board and leave it there for students to see each day, or you can "ditto" copies for each student to have. In either case, you should advise students to become very familiar with the reading assignments so they know what is expected of them.

Extra Activities Center   The Unit Resource Materials portion of this unit contains suggestions for a library of related books and articles in your classroom as well as crossword and word search puzzles. Make an extra activities center in your room where you will keep these materials for students to use. (Bring the books and articles in from the library and keep several copies of the puzzles on hand.) Explain to students that these materials are available for students to use when they finish reading assignments or other class work early.

Nonfiction Assignment Sheet   Explain to students that they each are to read at least one non-fiction piece from the in-class library at some time during the unit. Students will fill out a nonfiction assignment sheet after completing the reading to help you evaluate their reading experiences and to help the students think about and evaluate their own reading experiences.

Books   Each school has its own rules and regulations regarding student use of school books. Advise students of the procedures that are normal for your school.

PROJECT ASSIGNMENT - *Cheaper By the Dozen*

In *Cheaper By the Dozen*, Dad is a great one for finding projects for himself or the kids to do. All of his projects are educational and most of them have some element of fun. Your assignment is to pick a project to complete within the next two weeks. The project can be one from the list below or it can be one of your own that you would like to do, as long as it is educational and requires thought and practice or planning.

Here are some suggested projects:
1. Get language records and learn some phrases in a foreign language.
2. Learn morse code.
3. Learn the about the constellations, stars and planets.
4. Try to learn to play a musical instrument (a song on the bells, piano or guitar, for example) or if you know how to play already, learn a totally new, challenging piece of music.
5. Try Dad's typing method found in Chapter 6 and learn to type.
6. Learn Dad's math short-cuts and be prepared to answer problems from your class.
7. Build a bird bath. Take pictures of the building process (including any mistakes!).
8. Take family portraits of your family.
9. Make a motion study movie.
10. Make a movie about your family or some subject that interests you.

In about two weeks you will be asked to demonstrate your project to the class. Your demonstration will be graded on originality, competency, and difficulty, and you will be given a grade for the actual presentation. The more interesting your presentation is, the better your grade will be. When planning your presentation, try to be like Dad and find an unusual way to involve or interest your audience.

LESSON TWO

Objectives:
1. To preview the study questions and vocabulary for chapter 1
1. To have students practice reading orally
2. To read chapter 1
3. To evaluate students' oral reading
4. To preview the study questions and vocabulary for chapter 2

Activity #1
Have students complete the prereading work for chapter 1 of *Cheaper By The Dozen*. They should review the study questions and do the required vocabulary work.

Activity #2
Have students read chapter 1 of *Cheaper By The Dozen* out loud in class. You probably know the best way to get readers within your class; pick students at random, ask for volunteers, or use whatever method works best for your group. If you have not yet completed an oral reading evaluation for your students this marking period, this would be a good opportunity to do so. Continue oral reading in class over the next couple of days until everyone's oral reading has been evaluated. Then, students may read silently for in-class reading assignments. An oral reading evaluation form is included with this unit for your convenience.

Activity #3
If time remains in class after the oral reading, students should preview the study questions and do the vocabulary work for chapter 2. If no time remains in class, students should do this assignment as homework and have it completed prior to the next class period.

ORAL READING EVALUATION *Cheaper By The Dozen*

Name _____ Class____ Date _____

SKILL	EXCELLENT	GOOD	AVERAGE	FAIR	POOR
Fluency	5	4	3	2	1
Clarity	5	4	3	2	1
Audibility	5	4	3	2	1
Pronunciation	5	4	3	2	1
_____	5	4	3	2	1
_____	5	4	3	2	1

Total _____   Grade _____

Comments:

LESSON THREE

Objectives
    1. To read chapter 2
    2. To evaluate students' oral reading
    3. To preview the study questions and do the vocabulary work for chapters 3-5

Activity #1
    Have students read chapter 2 orally in class. Continue the oral reading evaluations.

Activity #2
    If there is time left in the class period, students should preview the study questions for chapters 3-5 and do the vocabulary worksheet for those chapters. If no time remains in class, this assignment should be done at home prior to the next class period.

LESSON FOUR

Objective
    To read chapters 3-5

Activity
    Have students read chapters 3-5 in class. If you have completed the oral reading evaluations, students may read silently.
    Having silent reading helps students practice concentrating on their own work even though they are in a large group. It also "speeds up" the reading of the novel, gives students a break from the monotony which sometimes develops with oral reading (particularly in slower classes), and encourages students' imaginations.
    If this assignment is not completed in class, students should complete reading these sections prior to the next class period.

LESSON FIVE

Objectives
    1. To review the main ideas and events in chapters 1-5 of *Cheaper By The Dozen*
    2. To help students get started on their unit projects, choose a project, and organize it
    3. Students will practice writing to inform
    4. Teachers will evaluate students' writing skills and see that their projects are appropriate

Activity #1
    Have students answer the study guide questions for chapters 1-5. Allow time for any necessary discussion. Write the correct answers on the board or overhead projector so students can copy them down for study use.

    Teacher's Note: Depending on the students' level, I have let different students write the answers on the board or even ask the questions to lead the group discussion. I would then jump in as necessary to guide the discussion. Use whatever techniques your particular group will handle best.

Activity #2
    Distribute Writing Assignment #1 and discuss the directions in detail. Give students the remainder of this class period to work on the assignment, and tell them on what day and date the composition is due.

NOTE: A writing evaluation form is included for your convenience. You may use the form when grading students' writing assignments, in preparation for a writing conference, which you may schedule during Lesson 6 or Lesson 8 or Lesson 9, depending on how long it will take you to evaluate Writing Assignment #1 and prepare for the conferences.

WRITING ASSIGNMENT #1 - *Cheaper By The Dozen*

PROMPT
Take a few minutes to think about the project you are doing with this unit. Have you decided on a project yet? If not, now is the time to decide on something. Tell me what you have in mind, a little bit about the project you have chosen, and why you have chosen it.

PREWRITING
Fill out the Assignment 1 Prewriting Form.

DRAFTING
Write one good, full paragraph for each of the headings on the form.

PROMPT
After you have finished a rough draft of your composition, revise it yourself until you are happy with your work. Then, ask a student who sits near you to tell you what he/she likes best about your work, and what things he/she thinks can be improved. Take another look at your work keeping in mind your critic's suggestions, and make the revisions you feel are necessary.

PROOFREADING
Do a final proofreading of your paper double-checking your grammar, spelling, organization, and the clarity of your ideas.

SUBMISSION
Submit your composition with the Assignment 1 Prewriting Form stapled on top.

DUE DATE _____

WRITING ASSIGNMENT 1 PREWRITNG FORM
Cheaper By The Dozen

Name _____ Date _____ Class _____

WHAT ACTIVITIES DID YOU CONSIDER DOING, AND WHAT DID YOU DECIDE ON?

WHY DID YOU CHOOSE THIS ACTIVITY? (List 2 or 3 reasons.)

WHAT, EXACTLY, WILL YOU HAVE TO DO FOR YOUR PROJECT? (List the steps you will have to do to complete your project.)

WHAT DO YOU THINK YOU WILL LEARN OR GAIN FROM DOING THIS PROJECT? (List 2 or 3 benefits.)

WRITING EVALUATION FORM - *Cheaper By The Dozen*

Name _____ Date _____

Writing Assignment #1 for the *Cheaper By The Dozen* unit Grade _____

Circle One For Each Item:

Description (paragraph 1)	excellent	good	fair	poor
Plans (body paragraphs)	excellent	workable	fair	not realistic
Conclusion	excellent	good	fair	poor
Grammar:	excellent	good	fair	poor (errors noted)
Spelling:	excellent	good	fair	poor (errors noted)
Punctuation:	excellent	good	fair	poor (errors noted)
Legibility:	excellent	good	fair	poor

Strengths:

Weaknesses:

Comments/Suggestions:

LESSON SIX

<u>Objectives</u>
    1. To preview the study questions and do the vocabulary work for chapters 6-8
    2. To read chapters 6-8

<u>Activity #1</u>
    Have students read through the study questions for this section of the book.

<u>Activity #2</u>
    Students should take the rest of this class period to read chapters 6-8 of *Cheaper By The Dozen*. If they do not complete this assignment in class, they should do so prior to the next class period.

LESSON SEVEN

<u>Objectives</u>
    1. To review the main events and ideas in chapters 6-8
    2. To have students practice logical thinking
    3. To give students the opportunity to practice working together in a small group
    4. To let students experience the essence of Mr. Gilbreth's job
    5. To encourage students' creativity

<u>Activity #1</u>
    Discuss the study questions for chapters 6-8, as directed in Lesson 5 for chapters 1-5.

<u>Activity #2</u>
    Divide your class into groups of two or three students. Explain to students that their assignment is to do a "motion study" project. They should pick a process, break it down into its "therbligs," and find the most efficient way of organizing those therbligs.
    Here are some suggestions for processes for this assignment:
    a. The routine during the day for getting from class to class (including locker stops for appropriate books, etc.)
    b. The morning routine from the time they get up until they are out the door to go to school
    c. The process of reading, studying, and learning the contents of a chapter of a textbook
    d. If any of your students work, they could do a motion study of their own work
    e. The process of evacuating the school (or their own homes) in case of fire

    Students are not limited to these topics, they can do a motion study of anything that interests them. Have each group give a short, oral report about its motion study.

LESSON EIGHT

Objectives
1. To preview the study questions and do the vocabulary work for chapters 9-11
2. To read chapters 9-11
3. Students will consider the ideas concerning being "popular"
4. Students will practice their writing skills
5. Teachers will evaluate students' writing

Activity 1
Give students about fifteen minutes to preview the study questions and do the vocabulary work for chapters 9-11.

Activity #2
Distribute Writing Assignment #2 and discuss the directions in detail. In the interests of conservation, you may wish to write the assignment on the board rather than duplicating a copy of the assignment for each of your students. Be sure to let students know when this assignment is due.

Activity #2
Students who finish the writing assignment early should begin reading chapters 9-11. All students should complete reading chapters 9-11 prior to the next class meeting.

LESSON NINE

Objectives
1. To review the main events and ideas of chapters 9-11
2. To preview the study questions and do the vocabulary work for chapters 12-16
3. To read chapters 12-16

Activity #1
Discuss the study questions for chapters 9-11 as directed for previous study question discussions.

Activity #2
Give students the remainder of the class period to preview the study questions, do the vocabulary work and reading for chapters 12-16.

WRITING ASSIGNMENT #2
Cheaper By The Dozen

PROMPT
"Popular!" Dad roared. "Popular. That's all I hear. That's the magic word, isn't it? That's what's the matter with this generation. Nobody thinks about being smart, or clever, or sweet or even attractive. No, sir. They want to be skinny and flat-chested and popular. They'd sell their soul and body to be popular, and if you ask me a lot of them do."

This book was first published in 1949 and the events of the book took place prior to 1924. Your assignment is to state whether or not this quotation is true today and to explain how it is so or why it is not. Be specific in your answer. A complete essay is expected for this assignment.

PREWRITING
How important is it to be popular today? *Do* people go to great lengths to be popular? What specific examples can you think of that show people *do* go to great lengths to be popular? List several. What specific examples can you think of that show people do *not* go to great lengths to be popular? List several. What do *you* do? Do you work at being popular, or are you just yourself no matter what—or something in between?

DRAFTING
Write an introductory paragraph that starts with the quotation above. As your last sentences in the paragraph, state whether or not you think this statement is true today or not.

In the body of your composition, write paragraphs explaining each of the two or three best examples you thought of which support your statement (a total of two or three paragraphs in the body of your composition, one for each example). You may change the names of the people in your examples if you wish to protect their identities.

As a concluding paragraph, explain how you personally feel about popularity, and whether or not it affects your life in any meaningful way.

PROMPT
After you have finished a rough draft of your composition, revise it yourself until you are happy with your work. Then, ask a student who sits near you to tell you what he/she likes best about your work, and what things he/she thinks can be improved. Take another look at your work keeping in mind your critic's suggestions, and make the revisions you feel are necessary.

PROOFREADING
Do a final proofreading of your paper double-checking your grammar, spelling, organization, and the clarity of your ideas.

DUE DATE _____

LESSON TEN

Objectives
1. To discuss the main events and ideas from chapters 12-16
2. To complete the nonfiction reading assignment
3. To preview the study questions and do the vocabulary work for chapters 17-19
4. To read chapters 17-19

Activity #1
Discuss the study questions for chapters 12-16, as directed previously.

Activity #2
Take students to the library. Distribute the Nonfiction Reading Assignment Worksheets.
Explain that students are to choose a nonfiction topic related in some way to *Cheaper by the Dozen*, read at least two articles relating to that topic, and fill out the worksheet. Give students the remainder of the class time to complete this assignment.

NOTE: Some suggested topics: industrial engineering, business administration, education, automobiles, boating, astronomy, family planning, running a household, psychology, foreign languages, "how to" articles (how to build something, how to do something).

Activity #3
If students finish the assignment early, they should begin working on previewing the study questions, doing the vocabulary worksheet, and reading chapters 17-19. This assignment should be completed prior to the next class period.

LESSON ELEVEN

Objectives
1. To review the main events and ideas in chapters 17-19
2. Students will practice writing to persuade

Activity #1
Discuss the study questions for chapters 17-19 as directed previously.

Activity #2
Distribute Writing Assignment #3 and discuss the directions in detail. Be sure to tell students when the composition is due. Give students the remainder of this class period to work on the assignment.

NONFICTION ASSIGNMENT SHEET
(To be completed after reading the required nonfiction article)

Name _____ Date _____

Title of Nonfiction Read _____

Written By _____ Publication Date _____

I. Factual Summary: Write a short summary of the piece you read.

II. Vocabulary
    1. With which vocabulary words in the piece did you encounter some degree of difficulty?

    2. How did you resolve your lack of understanding with these words?

III. Interpretation: What was the main point the author wanted you to get from reading his work?

IV. Criticism
    1. With which points of the piece did you agree or find easy to accept? Why?

    2. With which points of the piece did you disagree or find difficult to believe? Why?

V. Personal Response: What do you think about this piece? OR How does this piece influence your ideas?

WRITING ASSIGNMENT #3
Cheaper By The Dozen

PROMPT

We are persuaded daily by our friends, our parents and teachers, advertisers, newspapers, and many other sources. Do you recognize when you're being persuaded? Someone who has really mastered the art of persuasion can persuade you without your even knowing you're being manipulated. When we're very young, we only resort to begging ("Please, please, pretty-please with sugar on top?"). Then we graduate to trading ("If you'll do X, I'll do Y"). Beyond that, there's logic ("You should do X because . . . .) and various degrees of finesse used to manipulate and motivate.

In *Cheaper By The Dozen* the children used various means to try to get Dad and Mother to let them do the things they wanted to do. Sometimes they were successful and sometimes not.

Your assignment is to write a persuasive letter to your parent(s) or guardian(s), persuading them to let you do something you want to do. If your parent(s) or guardian(s) always let you do what you want, and you don't see a need to compose this letter, you should write a letter to the principal or a public official convincing them to do something you want.

PREWRITING

What do you want? Is there something you've been trying to get your parent(s) or guardian(s) to agree to? Is there some issue you'd like your principal or public official to address? Jot down some topic ideas, then choose one to write about.

Consider your audience. What point of view does your audience have on the topic? Why? What would convince your audience to let you do or have what you want? What could be in it for them? Are there logical reasons you can use? Is there something you can trade–something they want you to do you have been reluctant to do, something you can do that would benefit them? Persuasion has a lot to do with understanding the person or people you're trying to persuade. You really have to get into their skin and think about what they like and want, and how doing what *you* want will benefit them. Jot down a few notes about what your audience likes and wants, and how getting what you want will benefit them.

Choose your best point(s) and organize them in a way you think will be most effective.

DRAFTING

Use a letter format, either personal or formal, depending on your audience. Write a short introductory paragraph letting your audience know the topic. There are so many different and creative ways to write this letter, that it's difficult to give specific drafting instructions. Be creative. Be persuasive. Get your point across. The peer proofreading step below is really important. You might have two or three of your classmates read your letter to get several different opinions on how successful your letter is and how it might be improved.

Cheaper By The Dozen Writing Assignment #3 Page 2

PROMPT
    After you have finished a rough draft of your letter, revise it yourself until you are happy with your work. Then, ask a student who sits near you to tell you what he/she likes best about your work, and what things he/she thinks can be improved. Get a couple of different opinions. Take another look at your work keeping in mind your critics' suggestions, and make the revisions you feel are necessary.

PROOFREADING
    Do a final proofreading of your paper double-checking your grammar, spelling, organization, and the clarity of your ideas.

DUE DATE _____

LESSONS TWELVE AND THIRTEEN

Objective
To discuss the novel on a deeper than direct-recall level

Activity #1
Choose the questions from the Extra Discussion Questions/Writing Assignments which seem most appropriate for your students. A class discussion of these questions is most effective if students have been given the opportunity to formulate answers to the questions prior to the discussion. To this end, you may either have all the students formulate answers to all the questions, divide your class into groups and assign one or more questions to each group, or you could assign one question to each student in your class. The option you choose will make a difference in the amount of class time needed for this activity.

Activity #2
After students have had ample time to formulate answers to the questions, begin your class discussion of the questions and the ideas presented by the questions. Be sure students take notes during the discussion so they have information to study for the unit test.

EXTRA DISCUSSION QUESTIONS/WRITING ASSIGNMENTS
Cheaper By The Dozen

Interpretive

1. From what point of view is the story told, and why is that important?

2. What is the setting, and what does it add to the story?

3. Based on the facts in the story, can you tell approximately in what year the story takes place? Does it matter? What things about this book are timeless–true no matter what the year is?

4. Give a character sketch of each of the children in the book, noting not only their age differences, but their distinct personality traits as well.

5. Frank Gilbreth, Sr. never set out to be a motion study man; he only meant to get a job as a bricklayer. What traits did Dad have that helped him become such a success?

6. We all have our good points and our bad points. What were Dad's best personality traits? What were his faults?

7. What made the Family Council work? Why was it a success instead of a failure?

Critical

8. Explain the significance of the title "*Cheaper By The Dozen*."

9. Explain the dedication of the book which reads, "To Dad who reared only twelve children and To Mother who reared twelve only children."

10. Compare and contrast Mother and Dad.

11. If the story had been written from Dad's point of view, how would that have changed the story and its effect?

12. In what ways did Dad's involvement at school affect the children's lives?

13. In what ways does this book show the "growing pains" of the children?

14. Describe the Gilbreths' writing style. How does it influence our perception of the story?

15. Who is the main character of the book? Defend your choice.

Cheaper By The Dozen Extra Discussion Questions page 2

<u>Critical/Personal Response</u>

16. How does this book reflect the era in which it was written?

17. *Cheaper By The Dozen* is a very short novel, could anything have been gained by including more scenes from the time before or after the events of the story? If so, what could have been added and for what purpose? If not, explain why not.

18. In what ways did Dad make education interesting and fun? Are those kinds of things appropriate for school, or are they best only done at home?

19. There are no significant symbols, no deep, hidden meanings in this book, yet the book is still a valuable classic. Why?

20. The children in this book had responsibilities. What were their responsibilities? What are yours?

21. Dad's work (and Mother's) was very much a part of the family's life. Should it have been? What was the ultimate effect of this fact? Suppose he had had some other occupation. Would that have worked as well?

22. The Saturday Review of Literature called this book ". . . Sound Americana." What does that mean? Justify their appraisal.

23. Describe the use of personification in this book. What effect did it have?

24. Describe the authors' relationship with their parents, judging from the tone of the book and the many comments made about their parents. How do you think that relationship was developed?

25. What did the name Foolish Carriage mean to Dad? How could the same name have applied to Dad with the same meaning?

26. What did Dad want to save time *for*? What would you save time for?

Cheaper By The Dozen Extra Discussion Questions page 3

Personal Response

27. What was the purpose of a chaperon, when did parents stop chaperoning their kids, and what effect has the lack of chaperons had on the teen-aged society in general? Is that effect good or bad?

28. When the family went west to visit the Mollers, Mother changed. She slipped back into her role as "the daughter." Do your parents do that when your grandparents are around, and/or do you think you will do that when you go back home later in life?

29. There are many facets to Mother's character. She is "mother," "wife," "daughter," "businesswoman," and more. Is this true for all people? Are we all more than one-sided people? If so, what are the main ingredients around which all these facets of our personalities are built?

30. What does it mean to be a parent? What do good parents do?

LESSON FOURTEEN

Objectives
    To review all of the vocabulary work done in this unit

Activity
    Choose one (or more) of the vocabulary review activities listed on the next page(s) and spend your class period as directed in the activity. Some of the materials for these review activities are located in the Extra Activities Packet in this unit.

VOCABULARY REVIEW ACTIVITIES

1. Divide your class into two teams and have an old-fashioned spelling or definition bee.

2. Give each of your students (or students in groups of two, three or four) a *Cheaper By The Dozen* Vocabulary Word Search Puzzle. The person (group) to find all of the vocabulary words in the puzzle first wins.

3. Give students a *Cheaper By The Dozen* Vocabulary Word Search Puzzle without the word list. The person or group to find the most vocabulary words in the puzzle wins.

4. Use a *Cheaper By The Dozen* Vocabulary Crossword Puzzle. Put the puzzle onto a transparency on the overhead projector (so everyone can see it), and do the puzzle together as a class.

5. Give students a *Cheaper By The Dozen* Vocabulary Matching Worksheet to do.

6. Divide your class into two teams. Use the *Cheaper By The Dozen* vocabulary words with their letters jumbled as a word list. Student 1 from Team A faces off against Student 1 from Team B. You write the first jumbled word on the board. The first student (1A or 1B) to unscramble the word wins the chance for his/her team to score points. If 1A wins the jumble, go to student 2A and give him/her a definition. He/she must give you the correct spelling of the vocabulary word which fits that definition. If he/she does, Team A scores a point, and you give student 3A a definition for which you expect a correctly spelled matching vocabulary word. Continue giving Team A definitions until some team member makes an incorrect response. An incorrect response sends the game back to the jumbled-word face off, this time with students 2A and 2B. Instead of repeating giving definitions to the first few students of each team, continue with the student after the one who gave the last incorrect response on the team. For example, if Team B wins the jumbled-word face-off, and student 5B gave the last incorrect answer for Team B, you would start this round of definition questions with student 6B, and so on. The team with the most points wins!

LESSONS FIFTEEN AND SIXTEEN

Objectives
1. To evaluate students' Project Assignments
2. To give students practice at public speaking/performance

Activity
Have students each show or perform their projects for the entire class. Be sure to have made arrangements to have available any audio-visual equipment that students may need.

I have allowed two class periods for the project evaluations. The exact time needed will be determined by your class size, the kinds of projects your students have chosen, and the time limit (if any) you have imposed for each presentation.

LESSON SEVENTEEN

Objective:
To review the main events and ideas of *Cheaper By The Dozen*

Activity
Choose one of the review games/activities included in this packet and spend the remainder of your class time as outlined there.

Activity #3
Remind students of the unit test in the next class meeting. Stress the review of the study guides and their class notes as a last minute, brush-up review.

REVIEW GAMES/ACTIVITIES - *Cheaper By The Dozen*

1. Ask the class to make up a unit test for *Cheaper By The Dozen*. The test should have 4 sections: matching, true/false, short answer, and essay. Students may use 1/2 period to make the test and then swap papers and use the other 1/2 class period to take a test a classmate has devised. (open book) You may want to use the unit test included in this packet or take questions from the students' unit tests to formulate your own test.

2. Take 1/2 period for students to make up true and false questions (including the answers). Collect the papers and divide the class into two teams. Draw a big tic-tac-toe board on the chalk board. Make one team X and one team O. Ask questions to each side, giving each student one turn. If the question is answered correctly, that students' team's letter (X or O) is placed in the box. If the answer is incorrect, no mark is placed in the box. The object is to get three marks in a row like tic-tac-toe. You may want to keep track of the number of games won for each team.

3. Take 1/2 period for students to make up questions (true/false and short answer). Collect the questions. Divide the class into two teams. You'll alternate asking questions to individual members of teams A & B (like in a spelling bee). The question keeps going from A to B until it is correctly answered, then a new question is asked. A correct answer does not allow the team to get another question. Correct answers are +2 points; incorrect answers are -1 point.

4. Have students pair up and quiz each other from their study guides and class notes.

5. Give students a *Cheaper By The Dozen* crossword puzzle to complete.

6. Divide your class into two teams. Use the *Cheaper By The Dozen* word list words with their letters jumbled as a word list. Student 1 from Team A faces off against Student 1 from Team B. You write the first jumbled word on the board. The first student (1A or 1B) to unscramble the word wins the chance for his/her team to score points. If 1A wins the jumble, go to student 2A and give him/her a clue. He/she must give you the correct word which matches that clue. If he/she does, Team A scores a point, and you give student 3A a clue for which you expect another correct response. Continue giving Team A clues until some team member makes an incorrect response. An incorrect response sends the game back to the jumbled-word face off, this time with students 2A and 2B. Instead of repeating giving clues to the first few students of each team, continue with the student after the one who gave the last incorrect response on the team. For example, if Team B wins the jumbled-word face-off, and student 5B gave the last incorrect answer for Team B, you would start this round of clue questions with student 6B, and so on.

LESSON EIGHTEEN

Objective
> To test the students understanding of the main ideas and themes in *Cheaper By The Dozen*

Activity #1
> Distribute the unit tests. Go over the instructions in detail and allow the students the entire class period to complete the exam.

Activity #2
> Collect all test papers and assigned books prior to the end of the class period.

NOTES ABOUT THE UNIT TESTS IN THIS UNIT:

There are 5 different unit tests which follow.

There are two short answer tests which are based primarily on facts from the novel.

There is one advanced short answer unit test. It is based on the extra discussion questions and quotations. Use the matching key for short answer unit test 2 to check the matching section of the advanced short answer unit test. There is no key for the short answer questions and quotations. The answers will be based on the discussions you have had during class.

There are two multiple choice unit tests. Following the two unit tests, you will find an answer sheet on which students should mark their answers. The same answer sheet should be used for both tests; however, students' answers will be different for each test. Following the students answer sheet for the multiple choice tests you will find your answer keys.

The short answer tests have a vocabulary section. You should choose 10 of the vocabulary words from this unit, read them orally and have the students write them down. Then, either have students write a definition or use the words in sentences.

Use these words for the vocabulary section of the advanced short answer test:

ascertain	intricacies	inaugurated
inevitable	contagious	atrocious
conceded	ridicule	ludicrous
		philanthropy

UNIT TESTS

SHORT ANSWER UNIT TEST 1 *Cheaper by the Dozen*

I. Matching/Identification   Directions: Place the letter of the matching definition on the blank line.

_____ 1. Frank   A. Mother

_____ 2. Motorcycle Mac   B. canary

_____ 3. Lillian   C. Foolish Carriage

_____ 4. Pierce Arrow   D. the boat

_____ 5. Bill   E. the imitator

_____ 6. Moby Dick   F. Dad

_____ 7. Rena   G. the oldest Gilbreth child

_____ 8. Peter Soil   H. didn't escape tonsillectomy after all

_____ 9. Anna   I. the typewriter

_____ 10. Martha   J. was caught in the cherry tree

II. Short Answer
1. Describe Dad.

2. Describe Dad's relationship with the car.

Short Answer Unit Test 1 *Cheaper by the Dozen*

3. What did Dad do during an "Unavoidable Delay"?

4. How did Dad get started in the motion study business?

5. Why was the family council set up?

6. What was "of general interest"?

Short Answer Unit Test 1 *Cheaper by the Dozen*

7. Why did Dad go to school? What did he do there?

8. Who were the Mollers? Generally describe them.

9. What is a Therblig?

10. Why was Dad sad after Jane's birth?

Short Answer Unit Test 1 *Cheaper by the Dozen*

III. Quotations: Identify the speaker and discuss the significance of the following quotations.

1. "She's too young to try to paint that fence all by herself."

2. "I give nightly praise to my Maker that I never cast a ballot to bring that lazy, disreputable, ill-tempered beast into what was once my home."

3. "That's not one of ours, dear. He belongs next door."

4. "We're all going to be so proud of you today, dears. I know you're going to make such a lovely impression on all the guests."

5. "Somebody is kicking me, and I intend to get to the bottom of it. Literally."

Short Answer Unit Test 1 *Cheaper by the Dozen*

<u>IV. Essay</u>
    In what ways is *Cheaper by the Dozen* a tribute to Frank Gilbreth, Sr.?

Short Answer Unit Test 1 *Cheaper by the Dozen*

V. Vocabulary Part I
   Listen to the vocabulary word and spell it. After you have spelled all the words, go back and write down the definitions.

WORD   DEFINITION

1. _____   _____

2. _____   _____

3. _____   _____

4. _____   _____

5. _____   _____

6. _____   _____

7. _____   _____

8. _____   _____

9. _____   _____

10. _____   _____

Vocabulary Part 2: Place the letter of the matching definition on the blank line.

___ 1. Gall   A. a reward offered to motive one to action
___ 2. Unrequited   B. an emotion of respect and wonder tinged with fear
___ 3. Fraught   C. came to the edge of
___ 4. Ensue   D. make fun of
___ 5. Innuendoes   E. self-assertiveness
___ 6. Verged   F. disaster
___ 7. Incentive   G. not returned
___ 8. Ridicule   H. follow immediately afterward
___ 9. Awe   I. accompanied
___ 10. Debacle   J. things (usually negative) implied or suggested

ANSWER KEY SHORT ANSWER UNIT TEST 1 Cheaper by the Dozen

I. Matching/Identification
Directions: Place the letter of the matching definition on the blank line.

F   1. Frank   A. Mother

J   2. Motorcycle Mac   B. canary

A   3. Lillian   C. Foolish Carriage

C   4. Pierce Arrow   D. the boat

E   5. Bill   E. the imitator

I   6. Moby Dick   F. Dad

D   7. Rena   G. the oldest Gilbreth child

B   8. Peter Soil   H. didn't escape tonsillectomy after all

G   9. Anna   I. the typewriter

H 10. Martha   J. was caught in the cherry tree

II Short Answer
1. Describe Dad.
   Dad was a tall, large man who was an efficiency expert. He ran his home like a factory and cut all wasted time from anything. Although he ran his home in a business-like way, he also loved practical jokes, had a good sense of humor, and gave a great deal of his time to his family.
2. Describe Dad's relationship with the car.
   Dad loved Foolish Carriage. He drove the car "fast" and recklessly, and he loved every minute of it.
3. What did Father do during an "Unavoidable Delay"?
   He would take the time to find something to teach the children.
4. How did Father get started in the motion study business?
   He began as a bricklayer's helper, but kept finding ways that the bricklaying could be done better. He kept being promoted in the bricklaying company, and then he branched out to help other businesses do their work more efficiently.
5. Why was the family council set up?
   The cook and the handyman had too much work to do, so Mother and Father decided to divide the extra work among the kids. As "employers" and "employees," the parents and children decided to set up the council as a forum for making decisions and voicing

grievances.

6. What was "of general interest"?
   Talking at the dinner table was only allowed if the topic was of general interest. Decisions about whether or not a topic was of general interest were made by Dad, who usually overruled any "kid talk" and allowed all of the talk about his work, which the kids often found boring.
7. Why did Father go to school? What did he do there?
   He would pop in at the kids' classrooms to talk with their teachers and check on their progress. Often he would interrupt the schedule and disobey the school rules, but the teachers didn't seem
   to mind. They liked Mr. Gilbreth because he was so personable.
8. Who were the Mollers? Generally describe them.
   The Mollers were Mother's family; Moller was her maiden name. They were very wealthy and sugary sweet, addressing everyone as "Dear" so-and-so. The children thought that the Mollers were the "kissingest kin" in the world.
9. What is a Therblig?
   It is a unit of motion or thought, the basic unit on which Dad's business was built.
10. Why was Father sad after Jane's birth?
    He knew that there would be no more "latest models" in the Gilbreth family; there would be no more babies.

III. Quotations

1. "She's too young to try to paint that fence all by herself."
Mother said this to Dad about Lill. He had told the children to bid on the job of painting the fence. Lill was the lowest bidder. She was also the youngest child and Mother did not think she could handle the job.

2. "I give nightly praise to my Maker that I never cast a ballot to bring that lazy, disreputable, ill-tempered beast into what was once my home."
Dad said this about the dog. The Family Council voted to get the dog, but Dad never liked it.

3. "That's not one of ours, dear. He belongs next door."
Mother said this to Dad. She had been away on a business trip. When she returned he told her that most of the children had behaved, but that he had spanked one of the children. Dad pointed him out and Mother said he was not one of their children.

4. "We're all going to be so proud of you today, dears. I know you're going to make such a lovely impression on all the guests."
The aunts said this to the children. They were in California visiting Mother's family and this was the first time the children were going to be introduced to the friends and other relatives.

5. "Somebody is kicking me, and I intend to get to the bottom of it. Literally."
Aunt Anne said this. She was a guest at the dinner table. Bill was under the table, licking her hand and pretending to be a dog.

IV. Essay
   In what ways is *Cheaper by the Dozen* a tribute to Frank Gilbreth, Sr.?

   Grade this essay according to your own criteria.

V. Vocabulary Part I
Choose the words you want to use and write them in below.

WORD						DEFINITION
1. _____		_____
2. _____		_____
3. _____		_____
4. _____		_____
5. _____		_____
6. _____		_____
7. _____		_____
8. _____		_____
9. _____		_____
10. _____		_____

Vocabulary Part 2

E 1. Gall   A. a reward offered to motive one to action
G 2. Unrequited   B. an emotion of respect and wonder tinged with fear
I 3. Fraught   C. came to the edge of
H 4. Ensue   D. make fun of
J 5. Innuendoes   E. self-assertiveness
C 6. Verged   F. disaster
A 7. Incentive   G. not returned
D 8. Ridicule   H. follow immediately afterward
B 9. Awe   I. accompanied
F 10. Debacle   J. things (usually negative) implied or suggested

SHORT ANSWER UNIT TEST 2 Cheaper by the Dozen

I. Matching/Identification
Directions: Place the letter of the matching definition on the blank line.

_____ 1. Ernestine   A. family friend with 8 children

_____ 2. Mrs. Murphy   B. the photographer

_____ 3. Jane   C. code for "the bathroom"

_____ 4. Mrs. Cunningham   D. Dad's first job

_____ 5. Tom Grieves   E. the cook

_____ 6. Mr. Coggin   F. starting birth control chapter in town

_____ 7. Bricklayer   G. Mother's job

_____ 8. Psychologist   H. the handyman

_____ 9. Mrs. Mebane   I. the baby

_____ 10. Mrs. Bruce   J. had her tonsils out but didn't need to

II. Short Answer
1. What joke did Dad play on the children with the new car?

2. Why didn't Dad enter the Massachusetts Institute of Technology?

Short Answer Unit Test 2 *Cheaper by the Dozen*

3. Why did Lill paint the fence?

4. Why did Dad bring home the typewriter?

5. Why did Dad encourage Sunday School, even though he was not religious?

6. How did Mother change when she went home to the Mollers?

Short Answer Unit Test 2 *Cheaper by the Dozen*

7. How did Dad teach the children Morse Code?

8. What was Mother's reaction whenever Dad resorted to corporal punishment?

9. How did Anne get her parents to consent to letting the girls have their hair bobbed?

10. What was wrong with Dad?

Short Answer Unit Test 2 *Cheaper by the Dozen*

III. Quotations

Directions: Identify the speaker and discuss the significance of each of the following quotations.

1. "Do you want to try it? Can you run the house and take care of things until I get back?

2. "Say, Boss, on the way down here I had an idea about saving motions on packing those soapflakes for Lever Brothers. See what you think . . . ."

3. "It's all right, Mother. We've trapped a skunk up in the cherry tree, and we're trying to make him come down."

4. "Come on, Cinderella, before the good fairy turns things into field mice and pumpkins."

5. "I've taken many a picture of the 'ell in your 'ouse. But this will be the first time I've taken one of the 'ell on your 'ouse."

Short Answer Unit Test 2 *Cheaper by the Dozen*

IV: Essay
　　How did Mother change after Dad's death? How did this affect the family?

Short Answer Unit Test 2 *Cheaper by the Dozen*

V. Vocabulary Part I
Listen to the vocabulary word and spell it. After you have spelled all the words, go back and write down the definitions.

WORD   DEFINITION

1. _____   _____
2. _____   _____
3. _____   _____
4. _____   _____
5. _____   _____
6. _____   _____
7. _____   _____
8. _____   _____
9. _____   _____
10. _____   _____

Vocabulary Part 2
Directions: Place the letter of the matching definition on the blank line.

____ 1. regimentation   A. admitted; acknowledged as true

____ 2. ominously   B. social outcasts

____ 3. peril   C. uniformity and discipline

____ 4. benevolent   D. person with exceptional talents

____ 5. contagious   E. danger

____ 6. caucus   F. savage fierceness

____ 7. prodigy   G. tending to spread from one to another

____ 8. conceded   H. threateningly

____ 9. derelicts   I. meeting to decide questions of policy

____ 10. ferocity   J. kind; charitable

ANSWER KEY SHORT ANSWER UNIT TEST 2 *Cheaper by the Dozen*

I. Matching/Identification
Directions: Place the letter of the matching definition on the blank line.

J 1. Ernestine   A. family friend with 8 children

C 2. Mrs. Murphy   B. the photographer

I 3. Jane   C. code for "the bathroom"

E 4. Mrs. Cunningham   D. Dad's first job

H 5. Tom Grieves   E. the cook

B 6. Mr. Coggin   F. starting birth control chapter in town

D 7. Bricklayer   G. Mother's job

G 8. Psychologist   H. the handyman

F 9. Mrs. Mebane   I. the baby

A 10. Mrs. Bruce   J. had her tonsils out but didn't need to

II. Short Answer
1. What joke did Dad play on the children with the new car?
   He took each child alone to the car and told each one to find the birdie in the engine. He waited for each child to start looking in the engine, and then he honked the horn.

2. Why didn't Dad enter the Massachusetts Institute of Technology?
   He didn't want to drain his widowed mother's finances or interfere with his sister's studies

3. Why did Lill paint the fence?
   According to the council's rules, the person who submitted the lowest bid for doing a special job was awarded that job. Lill agreed to paint the fence for much less than the other children; she wanted to earn money for some skates. Even though the bid was ridiculously low and the job was very difficult for little Lill, Dad held her to her contract. (Although, he did buy her a new pair of skates when she finished the fence.)

4. Why did Dad bring home the typewriter?
   He had just invented a way for people to learn to type, and he wanted his kids to take advantage of his new system and to learn to type.

Answer Key Short Answer Unit Test 2 *Cheaper by the Dozen*

5. Why did Dad encourage Sunday School, even though he was not religious?
    He believed that a successful man knows something about everything. He wanted his children to have a well-rounded education, so he sent them to Sunday School to learn about religion and the Bible.

6. How did Mother change when she went home to the Mollers?
    She became a little girl again, forgetting about her career and responsibilities, and letting her parents make all the decisions for her.

7. How did Dad teach the children Morse Code?
    He left coded messages painted on the walls. The messages were often clues to the whereabouts of nice surprises, so the children would want to take the time to decode them.

8. What was Mother's reaction whenever Dad resorted to corporal punishment?
    She would always object to the part of the anatomy on which the punishment would have been inflicted.

9. How did Anne get her parents to consent to letting the girls have their hair bobbed?
    She bobbed her own and cried when it was criticized.

10. What was wrong with Dad?
    He had a bad heart. He had known about his bad heart for quite some time, but his health was obviously failing.

III. Quotations

1. "Do you want to try it? Can you run the house and take care of things until I get back?"
Mother asked this of the children soon after Dad died. She wanted to go on the business trip he had planned and give the talk he had prepared.

2. "Say, Boss, on the way down here I had an idea about saving motions on packing those soapflakes for Lever Brothers. See what you think . . . . "
This was Dad's last phone call to Mother. He had gone to the store, and called her from the pay phone. While they were on the phone Mother heard a thud, and the line went silent. Dad had died.

3. "It's all right, Mother. We've trapped a skunk up in the cherry tree, and we're trying to make him come down."
Anne said this. They had trapped Motorcycle Mac, one of Ernestine's admirers, in the cherry tree. He had climbed it hoping to get a glimpse of her. They were pretending they were going to set the tree on fire when Mother found them. After Anne's comment, Mother went back in the house.

Answer Key Short Answer Unit Test 2 *Cheaper by the Dozen*

4. "Come on, Cinderella, before the good fairy turns things into field mice and pumpkins."
Joe Scales, Anne's date for a school dance, said this to her. Dad had originally planned to go along on the date, but his car would not start and he refused to ride in Joe's car.

5. "I've taken many a picture of the 'ell in your 'ouse. But this will be the first time I've taken one of the 'ell on your 'ouse."
Mr. Coggins, the photographer, said this to Dad.

IV: Essay
How did Mother change after Father's death? How did this affect the family?

Grade the essay according to your own criteria.

V. Vocabulary Part I
Write the words and definitions you choose here, if you wish.

WORD   DEFINITION
1. _____   _____
2. _____   _____
3. _____   _____
4. _____   _____
5. _____   _____
6. _____   _____
7. _____   _____
8. _____   _____
9. _____   _____
10. _____   _____

Vocabulary Part 2

C 1. regimentation   A. admitted; acknowledged as true
H 2. ominously   B. social outcasts
E 3. peril   C. uniformity and discipline
J 4. benevolent   D. person with exceptional talents
G 5. contagious   E. danger
I 6. caucus   F. savage fierceness
D 7. prodigy   G. tending to spread from one to another
A 8. conceded   H. threateningly
B 9. derelicts   I. meeting to decide questions of policy
F 10. ferocity   J. kind; charitable

ADVANCED SHORT ANSWER TEST *Cheaper by the Dozen*

I. Matching/Identification

___ 1. Ernestine   A. family friend with 8 children

___ 2. Mrs. Murphy   B. the photographer

___ 3. Jane   C. code for "the bathroom"

___ 4. Mrs. Cunningham   D. Dad's first job

___ 5. Tom Grieves   E. the cook

___ 6. Mr. Coggin   F. starting birth control chapter in town

___ 7. Bricklayer   G. Mother's job

___ 8. Psychologist   H. the handyman

___ 9. Mrs. Mebane   I. the baby

___10. Mrs. Bruce   J. had her tonsils out but didn't need to

II. Short Answer

1. Explain why Dad did the following things: bought the Victrolas; brought home the typewriter; bought the *Rena*; hired someone to take movies of the children's tonsillectomies.

2. Describe what Dad did when the girls started dating. Use examples from the book.

Advanced Short Answer Test *Cheaper by the Dozen*

3. In what ways is *Cheaper by the Dozen* a tribute to Frank Gilbreth, Sr.?

4. What did the children do to the psychologist?

5. How did Mother change after Dad's death? How did this affect the family?

Advanced Short Answer Test *Cheaper by the Dozen*

III. Quotations
Directions: Identify the speaker and discuss the significance of each quotation.

1. "Say, Boss, on the way down here I had an idea about saving motions on packing those soapflakes for Lever Brothers. See what you think . . .."

2. "I give nightly praise to my Maker that I never cast a ballot to bring that lazy, disreputable, ill-tempered beast into what was once my home."

3. "Do you want to try it? Can you run the house and take care of things until I get back?

4. "I'll save you for last, Old Pioneer. The best for the last. Since the first day I laid eyes on your great, big, beautiful tonsils, I knew I wouldn't be content until I got my hands on them."

5. "The fifth."

Advanced Short Answer Test *Cheaper by the Dozen*

6. "I can't tell you how much I enjoyed seeing the dear folks. But the next time, you take the children out West, and I'll go to war."

7. "They don't act the way I pictured them. From your letters, I thought they whooped and hollered around. I don't believe they feel at home."

8. "For Lord's sake, Daddy. I feel just like a third wheel sitting in the back seat all by myself."

9. "Mr. Gilbreth, you're a sweet old duck."

10. "Christmas! Are you trying to burn me at the stake? Don't set fire to that. You'll roast me alive."

Advanced Short Answer Test *Cheaper by the Dozen*

<u>IV. Vocabulary</u>
Directions: Listen to the words and write them down. After you have written down all of the words, write a paragraph in which you use all the words. The paragraph must in some way relate to the book *Cheaper by the Dozen.*

MULTIPLE CHOICE UNIT TEST 1 *Cheaper by the Dozen*

I. Matching/Identification

___1. Frank   A. Mother

___2. Motorcycle Mac   B. was caught in cherry tree

___3. Lillian   C. the canary

___4. Pierce Arrow   D. the boat

___5. Bill   E. Foolish Carriage

___6. Moby Dick   F. Dad

___7. Rena   G. the oldest Gilbreth child

___8. Anna   H. didn't escape the tonsillectomy after all

___9. Peter Soil   I. the typewriter

___10. Martha   J. the imitator

II. Multiple Choice

1. What does Dad look like?
    A. He is tall and thin.
    B. He is short and heavy.
    C. He is tall and heavy.
    D. He is short and thin.

2. True or False: Dad ran his home like a factory and cut wasted time from everything.
    A. True
    B. False

3. What did Dad do during an "Unavoidable Delay"?
    A. He would take a nap.
    B. He would sing.
    C. He would read a book.
    D. He would teach the children something.

Multiple Choice Unit Test 1 *Cheaper by the Dozen*

4. What field of work was Dad in?
   A. motion study
   B. architect
   C. medicine
   D. farmer

5. How did the family make decisions and voice grievances?
   A. The parents made all decisions and did not listen to complaints.
   B. They set up a Family Council.
   C. The younger children told the older ones and they spoke with the parents.
   D. Everyone did what they wanted to do.

6. Talking at the dinner table was allowed only if the topic was of general interest. What did Dad consider to be general interest?
   A. politics
   B. current events
   C. family happenings
   D. his work

7. Father would often check on the children's progress at school. How did the teachers respond to him coming in and interrupting their classes?
   A. They didn't mind because they liked him.
   B. They locked their doors and told him to stay out.
   C. They put him to work.
   D. They threatened to fail the children if he didn't stop coming in.

8. Who were the Mollers?
   A. They were the hired couple who did the gardening and cooking.
   B. They were Dad's family.
   C. They were Mother's family.
   D. They were Dad's business partners.

9. A ____ is a unit of motion or thought, the basic unit on which Dad's business was built.
   A. Kimchee
   B. Therblig
   C. Quark
   D. Nanosecond

10. True or False: Dad knew that Jane would be the last baby.
    A. True
    B. False

Multiple Choice Unit Test 1 *Cheaper by the Dozen*

III. Quotations   Match the two halves of each quotation.

___ 1. One reason he had so many children–there were twelve of us–

___ 2. Catch one young enough

___ 3. Frankly, Dad didn't drive our car well at all.

___ 4. Well, they come

___ 5. Right now is

___ 6. I give nightly praise to my Maker that I never

___ 7. "That's fine, Ernie," he said.

___ 8. "It seems to me that the people of this town

___ 9. "Lillie, dear, it's good to see you,

___10. If and when I die,

A. cheaper by the dozen, you know.

B. cast a ballot to bring that lazy, disreputable, ill-tempered beast into what was once my home.

C. "I believe I'll keep you."

D. and there's no limit to what you can teach.

E. and the dear children," they kept repeating.

F. have pulled my leg on two different occasions today."

G. was that he was convinced anything he and Mother teamed up on was sure to be a success.

H. But he did drive it fast.

I. the happiest time in the world.

J. I'd like my brain to go to Harvard, where they are doing those brain experiments you told me about.

Multiple Choice Unit Test 1 *Cheaper by the Dozen*

IV. Vocabulary Matching

____ 1. VERACITY   A. Exceptionally bad

____ 2. VERGED   B. Without speaking

____ 3. BENEVOLENT   C. Lazy

____ 4. INDOLENT   D. Truthfulness

____ 5. MOCK   E. Lasting forever

____ 6. BEDLAM   F. Demonstrate or point out

____ 7. CALLIOPE   G. To come between; interfere

____ 8. PRECISELY   H. To come forth from; come into sight

____ 9. AILING   I. Begged for urgently

____ 10. SULLEN   J. Exactly

____ 11. TACITLY   K. Ill; sick

____ 12. INDICATE   L. Noisy uproar and confusion

____ 13. PERPETUAL   M. Came to the edge of

____ 14. EMERGE   N. Showing ill-humor or resentment

____ 15. FATIGUING   O. Kind; charitable

____ 16. SUBSEQUENT   P. Imitation; false

____ 17. INTERVENE   Q. Tiring

____ 18. IMPLORED   R. Following in order

____ 19. ATROCIOUS   S. Tending to spread from one to another

____ 20. CONTAGIOUS   T. Musical keyboard fitted with steam whistles

ANSWER SHEET KEY Multiple Choice Unit Test 1 *Cheaper by the Dozen*

I. Matching	III. Quotations	IV. Vocabulary
1. _____	1. _____	1. _____
2. _____	2. _____	2. _____
3. _____	3. _____	3. _____
4. _____	4. _____	4. _____
5. _____	5. _____	5. _____
6. _____	6. _____	6. _____
7. _____	7. _____	7. _____
8. _____	8. _____	8. _____
9. _____	9. _____	9. _____
10. _____	10. _____	10. _____
		11. _____
		12. _____
		13. _____
		14. _____
		15. _____
		16. _____
		17. _____
		18. _____
		19. _____
		20. _____

II. Multiple Choice

1. (A) (B) (C) (D)
2. (A) (B) (C) (D)
3. (A) (B) (C) (D)
4. (A) (B) (C) (D)
5. (A) (B) (C) (D)
6. (A) (B) (C) (D)
7. (A) (B) (C) (D)
8. (A) (B) (C) (D)
9. (A) (B) (C) (D)
10. (A) (B) (C) (D)

ANSWER SHEET KEY Multiple Choice Unit Test 1 *Cheaper by the Dozen*

I. Matching		III. Quotations		IV. Vocabulary	
1.	F	1.	G	1.	D
2.	B	2.	D	2.	M
3.	A	3.	H	3.	O
4.	E	4.	A	4.	C
5.	J	5.	I	5.	P
6.	I	6.	B	6.	L
7.	D	7.	C	7.	T
8.	G	8.	F	8.	J
9.	C	9.	E	9.	K
10.	H	10.	J	10.	N
				11.	B
				12.	F
				13.	E
				14.	H
				15.	Q
				16.	R
				17.	G
				18.	I
				19.	A
				20.	S

II. Multiple Choice

1. (A) (B) ( ) (D)
2. ( ) (B) (C) (D)
3. (A) (B) (C) ( )
4. ( ) (B) (C) (D)
5. (A) ( ) (C) (D)
6. (A) (B) (C) ( )
7. ( ) (B) (C) (D)
8. (A) (B) ( ) (D)
9. (A) ( ) (C) (D)
10. ( ) (B) (C) (D)

MULTIPLE CHOICE UNIT TEST 2 *Cheaper by the Dozen*

I. Matching/Identification

___ 1. Ernestine   A. family friend with 8 children

___ 2. Mrs. Murphy   B. the photographer

___ 3. Jane   C. code for "the bathroom"

___ 4. Mrs. Cunningham   D. Dad's first job

___ 5. Tom Grieves   E. the cook

___ 6. Mr. Coggin   F. starting birth control chapter in town

___ 7. Bricklayer   G. Mother's job

___ 8. Psychologist   H. the handyman

___ 9. Mrs. Mebane   I. the baby

___ 10. Mrs. Bruce   J. had her tonsils out but didn't need to

II. Multiple Choice

1. One time while Mother was away, Dad spanked one child to put him in line. What did Mother say about this when she returned?
    A. She was glad that Dad had disciplined the child.
    B. She was angry because she never spanked the children.
    C. She said that the disorderly child was not theirs; he was a neighbor.
    D. She said that she did not want to know what happened when she was away.

2. What was Dad's signal for everyone to gather?
    A. He whistled.
    B. He played a song on the trumpet.
    C. He rang a large bell.
    D. He turned on a siren.

Multiple Choice Unit Test 2 *Cheaper by the Dozen*

3. Which statement about the fence painting is true?
    A. Dad hired a professional painter and took the cost out of the children's' allowances.
    B. All of the children painted for free.
    C. Lil got the job because she was the lowest bidder.
    D. Mother painted it because she liked working outside.

4. Dad thought his children were not the same as children with average parents. What did he do to promote this idea?
    A. He started his own school for his children.
    B. He pushed for his children to skip grades at the public school.
    C. He gave the children extra assignments at home.
    D. He sent them to an exclusive private prep school.

5. How did the Mollers address everyone?
    A. "Sweetheart"
    B. "Hey, you"
    C. "Kiddo"
    D. "Dear"

6. What happened when the children finally decided to "feel at home" at the Mollers' house?
    A. They wrote on the bedroom walls with crayons.
    B. They put toilet paper all over the outside of the house.
    C. They hopped into the garden sprinklers and got wet.
    D. They all refused to eat dinner at the same time.

7. What did Dad say about sickness?
    A. It was a natural part of life.
    B. It gave a person time to rest and think.
    C. It was preventable with a proper life style.
    D. It dragged down the performance of the entire group.

Multiple Choice Unit Test 2 *Cheaper by the Dozen*

8. A ____ is a unit of motion or thought, the basic unit on which Dad's business was built.
   A. Kimchee
   B. Therblig
   C. Quark
   D. Nanosecond

9. What stunt did the children do when Dad got a job with an automatic pencil company?
   A. They all learned to write with their toes.
   B. They built a ten-foot tall pencil out of pencils.
   C. They gave out pencils to everyone in the school.
   D. They buried old wooden pencils in a coffin.

10. What did Mother do after Dad died?
   A. She moved the family to California to live with her parents.
   B. She went on with Dad's work.
   C. She went back to college.
   D. She became depressed and stayed in bed for six months.

Multiple Choice Unit Test 2 *Cheaper by the Dozen*

III. Quotations   Directions: Match the two parts of each quotation.

___ 1. "Do you want to try it?

___ 2. "It's all right, Mother.

___ 3. "I've taken many a picture of the 'ell in your 'ouse.

___ 4. "Say, Boss, on the way down here I had an idea about saving

___ 5. "I can't tell you how much I enjoyed seeing the dear folks.

___ 6. "Somebody is kicking me,

___ 7. "She's too young

___ 8. I give nightly praise to my Maker that I never

___ 9. "Mr. Gilbreth,

___10. They don't act the way I pictured them.

A. motions on packing those soapflakes for Lever Brothers. See what you think . . .."

B. and I intend to get to the bottom of it. Literally."

C. We've trapped a skunk up in the cherry tree, and we're trying to make him come down."

D. But this will be the first time I've taken one of the 'ell on your 'ouse."

E. cast a ballot to bring that lazy, disreputable, ill-tempered beast into what was once my home."

F. But the next time, you take the children out West, and I'll go to war."

G. to try to paint that fence all by herself."

H. you're a sweet old duck."

I. Can you run the house and take care of things until I get back?"

J. From your letters, I thought they whooped and hollered around. I don't believe they feel at home."

Multiple Choice Unit Test 2 *Cheaper by the Dozen*

IV. Vocabulary Part 1   Directions: Match the word and its meaning.
___ 1. dire   A. yielded; gave in
___ 2. repentant   B. disaster
___ 3. sullen   C. laughable because it's ridiculous or foolish
___ 4. invective   D. dislike intensely
___ 5. debacle   E. terrible; disastrous
___ 6. detest   F. kindly but seriously reprimanded
___ 7. intervene   G. showing ill-humor or resentment
___ 8. ludicrous   H. sorry for a wrong-doing
___ 9. capitulated   I. insults
___10. admonished   J. come between; interfere

Vocabulary Part 2 Directions: mark the letter next to the word that matches the definition.

11. a person authorized to act for another
    a. dire
    b. calliope
    c. proxy
    d. lurid

12. unavoidable; going to happen no matter what
    a. inanimate
    b. implied
    c. innuendoes
    d. inevitable

13. possessed in common
    a. delectable
    b. surreptitious
    c. mutual
    d. belligerent

14. following in order
    a. precluded
    b. subsequent
    c. fatalistic
    d. inadequate

15. released from entanglement
    a. abetted
    b. mutinous
    c. extricated
    d. ensconced

16. event preceding a more important one
    a. prelude
    b. optimist
    c. reprobates
    d. incentive

17. harmless
    a. fraught
    b. innocuous
    c. ludicrous
    d. fatiguing

18. giving charitable donations or aid
    a. conceded
    b. intrepidity
    c. demoralizing
    d. philanthropy

19. irritated; annoyed
    a. irked
    b. disheveled
    c. admonished
    d. insolent

20. not returned
    a. veracity
    b. unrequited
    c. mayhem
    d. agenda

ANSWER SHEET Multiple Choice Unit Test 2 Cheaper *by the Dozen*

I. Matching

1. _____
2. _____
3. _____
4. _____
5. _____
6. _____
7. _____
8. _____
9. _____
10. _____

II. Multiple Choice

1. (A) (B) (C) (D)
2. (A) (B) (C) (D)
3. (A) (B) (C) (D)
4. (A) (B) (C) (D)
5. (A) (B) (C) (D)
6. (A) (B) (C) (D)
7. (A) (B) (C) (D)
8. (A) (B) (C) (D)
9. (A) (B) (C) (D)
10. (A) (B) (C) (D)

III. Quotations

1. _____
2. _____
3. _____
4. _____
5. _____
6. _____
7. _____
8. _____
9. _____
10. _____

IV. Vocabulary

1. _____
2. _____
3. _____
4. _____
5. _____
6. _____
7. _____
8. _____
9. _____
10. _____
11. _____
12. _____
13. _____
14. _____
15. _____
16. _____
17. _____
18. _____
19. _____
20. _____

ANSWER SHEET KEY Multiple Choice Unit Test 2 Cheaper *by the Dozen*

I. Matching	III. Quotations	IV. Vocabulary
1. J	1. I	1. E
2. C	2. C	2. H
3. I	3. D	3. G
4. E	4. A	4. I
5. H	5. F	5. B
6. B	6. B	6. D
7. D	7. G	7. J
8. G	8. E	8. C
9. F	9. H	9. A
10. A	10. J	10. F
		11. C
		12. D
		13. C
		14. B
		15. C
		16. A
		17. B
		18. D
		19. A
		20. B

II. Multiple Choice

1. (A) (B) ( ) (D)
2. ( ) (B) (C) (D)
3. (A) (B) ( ) (D)
4. (A) ( ) (C) (D)
5. (A) (B) (C) ( )
6. (A) (B) ( ) (D)
7. (A) (B) (C) ( )
8. (A) ( ) (C) (D)
9. (A) (B) (C) ( )
10. (A) ( ) (C) (D)

UNIT RESOURCE MATERIALS

EXTRA ACTIVITIES

One of the difficulties in teaching a novel is that all students don't read at the same speed. One student who likes to read may take the book home and finish it in a day or two. Sometimes a few students finish the in-class assignments early. The problem, then, is finding suitable extra activities for students.

One thing that helps is to keep a little library in the classroom. For this unit on *Cheaper By The Dozen*, you might check out from the school library other related books and articles about industrial engineering, business administration, education, automobiles, boating, astronomy, family planning, running a household, psychology or foreign languages. "How to" books might interest some students.

The other things you may keep on hand are word search or crossword puzzles. We have made some of them relating directly to *Cheaper By The Dozen* for you. Feel free to duplicate them for your class.

Some students may like to draw. You might devise a contest or allow some extra-credit grade for students who draw characters or scenes from *Cheaper By The Dozen*. Note, too, that if the students do not want to keep their drawings you may pick up some extra bulletin board materials this way. If you have a contest and you supply the prize, you could, possibly, make the drawing itself a non-refundable entry fee.

MORE ACTIVITIES *Cheaper By The Dozen*

1. Have students design a book cover (front and back and inside flaps) for *Cheaper By The Dozen*.

2. Have students design a bulletin board (ready to be put up; not just sketched) for *Cheaper By The Dozen*.

3. Have students (either individually or in groups) determine the costs involved with supporting a family of 12 children for one year. Title your bulletin board CHEAPER BY THE DOZEN? and list all the costs your students suggest.

4. Use some of the related topics (noted earlier for an in-class library) as topics for research, reports or written papers, or as topics for guest speakers.

5. Have students compare family life in our society in the 1920s with family life today.

6. Have students write stories about their own families, imitating the light, humorous style that the Gilbreths used.

7. Have a "clean up" day during which your class cleans up the school grounds or a section of your neighborhood. (Dad had the kids pick up their trash and any other trash in the area after a picnic.)

BULLETIN BOARD IDEAS
Cheaper By The Dozen

1. Save one corner of the board for the best of students' writing assignments.

2. Take one of the word search puzzles from the extra activities packet and (with a marker) copy it over in a large size on the bulletin board. Write the clue words to one side. Invite students prior to and after class to find the words and circle them on the bulletin board.

3. See the introductory activity, Lesson One.

4. Do a bulletin board about the many careers suggested in this book. Provide information about education needed, demand for the position, salary, benefits, etc.

5. Do a bulletin board about education, showing education at school as just a part of a person's entire educational background (others being home, friends and relatives, work, reading, play time, television, etc.)

6. Divide your board into several sections, one devoted to each of the episodes in the book: boating, foreign language, photography, astronomy, etc.

7. See Extra Activity #3.

8. Do a bulletin board comparing family life in the 1920s to family life today.

JUGGLE LETTER REVIEW CLUES *Cheaper By The Dozen*

ANNE	NENA	She bobbed her hair
BATH	HABT	The bird ___ was Dad's only failure
BILL	LIBL	He made Aunt Anne furious by pretending to be a dog
BRICKLAYER	RCRBAYKELI	Father began work as a _____'s helper
BURTON	OUBNTR	Doctor who got Ernestine and Martha mixed up
CALIFORNIA	NALCFIROAI	State where Mollers lived
CANARIES	SCRIANEA	Peter and Maggie
CHEAPER	PCHERAE	____ By The Dozen
COFFIN	FCNIFO	The children buried one full of pencils
COGGIN	GONIGC	He forgot to take the lens cap off the camera, so there were no movies of the tonsillectomy
COUGH	UOHCG	All the children got the whooping ____ on the way home from CA
COUNCIL	OIULCCN	The family ___ was set up as a forum for making decisions & voicing grievances
EFFICIENCY	NFEYCCIIEF	Dad was an ____ expert
ERNESTINE	NRNEITEES	Co-author; _____ Gilbreth Carey
FLASH	SHAFL	It terrified the children when Father took pictures
FOOLISH	LHOOSIF	The car; ____ Carriage
GROSIE	SORGEI	She had power over mother; mother obeyed her
HEART	TRHEA	Dad had a bad one
JANE	NEAJ	The last baby
JAZZ	ZAZJ	Dad did not like the ___ Age
JINGO	OJGIN	Dad's saying; By ___!
JOE	OJE	He looked like what might happen if a pygmy married a barber pole.
KIN	NIK	The children thought the Mollers were the
LANGUAGE	GUNAGALE	The children studied recorded ____ lessons
LILL	LLLI	She underbid the others & painted the fence
MAC	CAM	Motorcycle ___ was caught peeping in Ernestine's window
MARTHA	RATHAM	She learned to do math quickly in her head
MEASLES	SLESAME	Father put red ink spots on his face, pretending to have ___
MEBANE	BAMEEN	She tried to organize a group of women to be advocates of birth control
MOLLERS	SLOELRM	They were Mother's family
MORSE	SOMER	Father painted messages on the walls in ___ code
MOTION	NMTIOO	Dad's occupation; ___ study
POOR	OORP	Over the hill and to the ___ house
PSYCHOLOGIST	GOOHILSSTCYP	The children tried to make him think they were horribly maladjusted

Cheaper By The Dozen Juggle Letter Review Clues Continued

RENA	NARE	The boat
SHOE	HOES	Name for the cottage
SUNDAY	YDANUS	The children went to ___ school because Mr. Gilbreth wanted them to have a well-rounded education
TEA	AET	At the ___ party the kids got tired of being angels & jumped into the sprinkler water
THERBLIG	LGBIHTRE	A unit of motion or thought
TONSILS	LOSSTNI	The children and Dad had theirs removed
TYPEWRITER	WETRYEPIRT	It was named Moby Dick
WHISTLE	SWELTHI	Signal for everyone to gather

WORD SEARCH *Cheaper By The Dozen*

Words are placed backwards, forward, diagonally, up and down. Words listed below are included in the maze. Circle the hidden vocabulary words in the maze.

```
M O T I O N H E A R T T H E R B L I G N
R V F M H J O N Z P S T S K H M L N F N
N F B G O J H A H I O B S N M B I H O P
C V U C G L N J G R M O I D L G B W O N
Y O R W O F L O C K E K R L G G N J L W
C S T Z C U L E V L A R I O V J X M I N
B C O C V O N V R X S L C H R I L O S S
R A N M H Z Y C P S L J G M M N M R H Y
X T T C B P C E I L E H C D G G C S S B
L Y Y H T O N S I L S J A Z Z O D E E V
M S X G V A E V P A H U B L F H N O G W
P A S F B Q I F L Z C Z N F R N H M J V
S K R E Q M C F M G H R I D A S W X Q T
C A M T W H I S T L E N E G A U G N A L
N N E Q H M F V N N A K R Y J Y F K S C
S A V G Q A F V A F P C A N A R I E S D
G R O S I E E E R N E S T I N E V X N Z
T Y P E W R I T E R R E Y A L K C I R B
```

ANNE	EFFICIENCY	LANGUAGE	RENA
BATH	ERNESTINE	LILL	SHOE
BILL	FLASH	MAC	SUNDAY
BRICKLAYER	FOOLISH	MARTHA	TEA
BURTON	GROSIE	MEASLES	THERBLIG
CANARIES	HEART	MEBANE	TONSILS
CHEAPER	JANE	MOLLERS	TYPEWRITER
COFFIN	JAZZ	MORSE	WHISTLE
COGGIN	JINGO	MOTION	
COUGH	JOE	POOR	
COUNCIL	KIN	PSYCHOLOGIST	

ANSWER KEY WORD SEARCH *Cheaper By The Dozen*

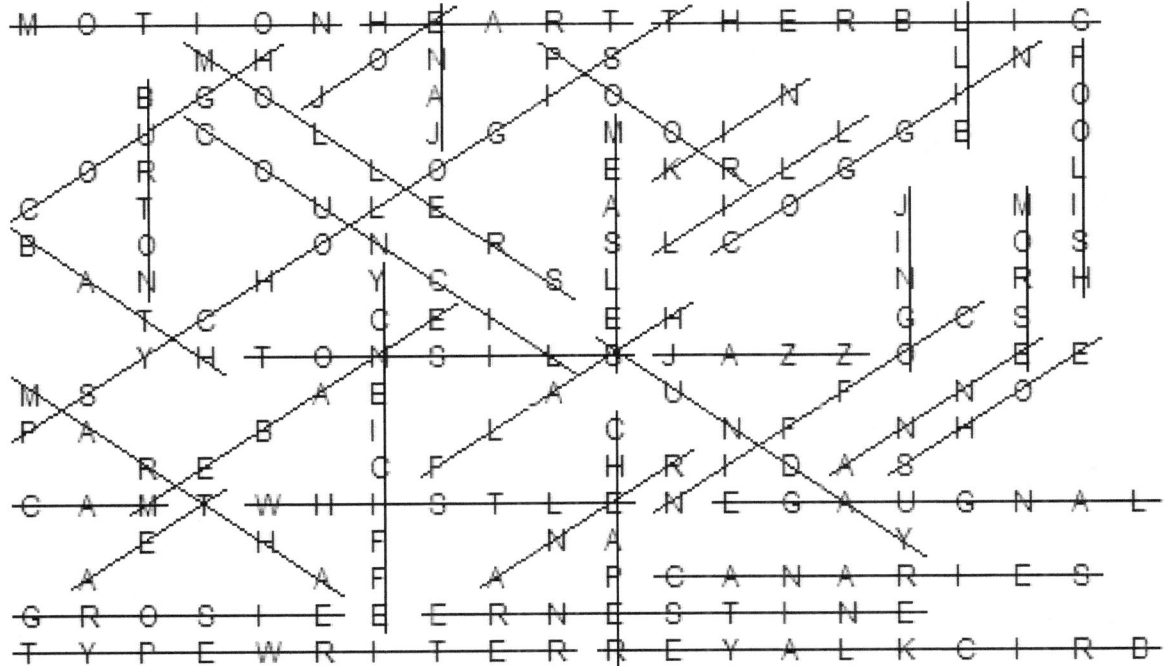

CROSSWORD *Cheaper By The Dozen*

132

CROSSWORD CLUES *Cheaper By The Dozen*

ACROSS
1 The children and Dad had theirs removed
4 Father put red ink spots on his face, pretending to have _____
7 State where Mollers lived
11 The children thought the Mollers were the kissingest ___ in the world
12 He made Aunt Anne furious by pretending to be a dog
13 The last baby
14 She bobbed her hair
17 The bird ___ was Dad's only failure
19 Over the hill and to the ___ house
20 He looked like what might happen if a pygmy married a barber pole
25 Dad's occupation: ___ study
26 She had power over Mother; Mother obeyed her
27 Father painted messages on the walls in ___ code
28 ___ By The Dozen

DOWN
1 At the ___ party the kids got tired of being angels & jumped into the sprinkler water
2 The children went to ___ school because Mr. Gilbreth wanted them to have a well-rounded education
3 Dad did not like the ___ Age
4 She learned to do math quickly in her head
5 The children studied recorded ___ lessons
6 Name for the cottage
7 He forgot to take the lens cap off the camera, so there were no movies of the tonsillectomy
8 She underbid the others & painted the fence
9 The car; ___ Carriage
10 The boat
13 Dad's saying: By ___
15 Co-author; ___ Gilbreth Carey
16 It was named Moby Dick
17 Father began work as a ___'s helper
18 A unit of motion or thought
21 Peter and Maggie
22 It terrified the children when Father took pictures
23 Doctor who got Ernestine and Martha mixed up
24 Signal for everyone to gather
24 Motorcycle ___ was caught peeping in Ernestine's window

CROSSWORD ANSWER KEY *Cheaper By The Dozen*

MATCHING 1 *Cheaper By The Dozen*

___ 1. TYPEWRITER   A. The children buried one full of pencils

___ 2. BRICKLAYER   B. The family ___ was set up as a forum for making decisions & voicing grievances

___ 3. CALIFORNIA   C. It terrified the children when Father took pictures

___ 4. MARTHA   D. ___ By The Dozen

___ 5. COFFIN   E. The children thought the Mollers were the kissingest ___ in the world

___ 6. LILL   F. She underbid the others & painted the fence

___ 7. FLASH   G. Dad was an ___ expert

___ 8. KIN   H. Father began work as a ___'s helper

___ 9. HEART   I. The children went to ___ school because Mr. Gilbreth wanted them to have a well-rounded education

___ 10. SUNDAY   J. She bobbed her hair

___ 11. MAC   K. She learned to do math quickly in her head

___ 12. SHOE   L. Name for the cottage

___ 13. POOR   M. Over the hill and to the ___ house

___ 14. EFFICIENCY   N. It was named Moby Dick

___ 15. JAZZ   O. State where Mollers lived

___ 16. TONSILS   P. Dad had a bad one

___ 17. ANNE   Q. The children tried to make him think they were horribly maladjusted

___ 18. CHEAPER   R. Dad did not like the ___ Age

___ 19. COUNCIL   S. Motorcycle ___ was caught peeping in Ernestine's window

___ 20. PSYCHOLOGIST T. The children and Dad had theirs removed

MATCHING 2 *Cheaper By The Dozen*

____ 1. TEA　　　　　　A. She had power over Mother; Mother obeyed her

____ 2. COGGIN　　　　B. The children thought the Mollers were the kissingest ___ in the world

____ 3. BRICKLAYER　　C. He forgot to take the lens cap off the camera, so there were no movies of the tonsillectomy

____ 4. MEASLES　　　D. Doctor who got Ernestine and Martha mixed up

____ 5. WHISTLE　　　E. Father put red ink spots on his face, pretending to have ___

____ 6. FOOLISH　　　F. They were Mother's family

____ 7. SUNDAY　　　G. The children went to ___ school because Mr. Gilbreth wanted them to have a well-rounded education

____ 8. FLASH　　　　H. Signal for everyone to gather

____ 9. BILL　　　　　I. The car; ____ Carriage

____ 10. GROSIE　　　J. He made Aunt Anne furious by pretending to be a dog

____ 11. KIN　　　　　K. Dad's occupation; ___ study

____ 12. MOLLERS　　L. Name for the cottage

____ 13. COUNCIL　　M. At the ___ party the kids got tired of being angels & jumped into the sprinkler water

____ 14. CANARIES　　N. Peter and Maggie

____ 15. SHOE　　　　O. Father began work as a _____'s helper

____ 16. JOE　　　　　P. It terrified the children when Father took pictures

____ 17. BURTON　　　Q. Dad was an ____ expert

____ 18. MOTION　　　R. The family ___ was set up as a forum for making decisions & voicing grievances

____ 19. EFFICIENCY　S. He looked like what might happen if a pygmy married a barber pole

____ 20. COFFIN　　　T. The children buried one full of pencils

WORKSHEET ANSWER KEYS *Cheaper By The Dozen*

	MATCH 1	MATCH 2
1	N	M
2	H	C
3	O	O
4	K	E
5	A	H
6	F	I
7	C	G
8	E	P
9	P	J
10	I	A
11	S	B
12	L	F
13	M	R
14	G	N
15	R	L
16	T	S
17	J	D
18	D	K
19	B	Q
20	Q	T

VOCABULARY RESOURCE MATERIALS

VOCABULARY WORD LIST *Cheaper By The Dozen*

This is a list of all the vocabulary words covered in this LitPlan.
It can serve as a list for any game you might want to devise.

ADMONISHED	DEHNISDAMO	Kindly but seriously reprimanded
AGENDA	EDANGA	List of things to be done
AILING	LAIGNI	Ill; sick
ALIAS	SLAIA	An assumed name
APPRECIATIVE	EARPEPVTICAI	Grateful
APTITUDE	PATTEDIU	Ability
ASCERTAIN	NASICAETR	Find out
ATROCIOUS	SCOUTRAOI	Exceptionally bad
AWE	WEA	An emotion of respect and wonder tinged with fear
BEDLAM	DALBME	Noisy uproar and confusion
BELLIGERENT	LEERETBIGNR	Aggressive; hostile
BENEVOLENT	TNEBNVEOLE	Kind; charitable
CALLIOPE	PALCIOLE	Musical keyboard fitted with steam whistles
CAPITULATED	UTLAIPTACDE	Yielded; gave in
CAUCUS	SCAUCU	A meeting to decide upon questions of policy
COINCIDE	DENCICOI	To happen at the same time
CONCEDED	DENOCEDC	Admitted; acknowledged as true
CONFERRED	RONFEEDCR	Bestowed or given as an honor
CONTAGIOUS	SAGOUTINOC	Tending to spread from one to another
CONVENT	NOVETCN	Home for nuns
CONVERGED	VODCNEREG	Approached the same point from different directions
CONVICTION	TOVOCININC	Strong belief
DEBACLE	BELEDAC	Disaster
DEBUTANTE	NABEDTTUE	Young woman who is formally presented to society
DELECTABLE	CADEELBLET	Enjoyable; delightful
DERELICTS	STIRECLED	Social outcasts
DETEST	STEDTE	Dislike intensely
DILEMMA	MAMILED	A situation requiring a choice
DIRE	REDI	Terrible; disastrous
DOCILE	CEDOLI	Obedient; submissive to management
DORY	YROD	Small, narrow, flat-bottomed boat
EMERGE	GEEMRE	To come forth from; come into sight
ENSCONCED	DONCEENSC	Settled securely
ENSUE	NEEUS	To follow immediately after
ENTAIL	LAITEN	To have a necessary accompaniment or consequences
EXTRICATE	TEXETCAIR	Release from entanglement
FATALISTIC	TCLIAFATSI	Belief that events are predetermined; submission to fate

Cheaper By The Dozen Word List Continued

FATIGUING	GFUNIGTAI	Tiring
FEROCITY	CFRETYIO	Savage fierceness
FORGO	OORGF	Give up
FRAUGHT	THARGUF	Accompanied by or filled with something undesirable
GALL	LAGL	Self-assertiveness
IMPLIED	DILPMIE	Suggested without directly saying
IMPLORED	PDORLEMI	Begged for urgently
INAUGURATED	GRTAEDUNAIU	Began
INCENTIVE	VECNNIEIT	A reward offered to motivate one to action
INCREDULOUSLY	DLLOUINERCYUS	Expressing disbelief
INDICATE	IETDNIAC	Demonstrate or point out
INDIGNANTLY	GNNDIINYALT	Angrily because of something unjust
INDOLENT	EOLNTIDN	Lazy
INEVITABLE	VBIEALTNIE	Unavoidable; going to happen no matter what
INNOCUOUS	CUUNINOOS	Harmless
INNUENDOES	SNUNIEEDON	Things (usually negative) implied or suggested
INTERVENE	NRVNIEETE	To come between; interfere
INTRICACIES	RICCTNASEII	Many complexly arranged elements
INVECTIVE	TEENVICIV	Insults
IRKED	KRIED	Irritated; annoyed
LUDICROUS	UIOUSRCDL	Laughable because it's ridiculous or foolish
LURID	DRUIL	Causing shock or horror
MOCK	KOCM	Imitation; false
MUTINOUS	SONTUMUI	Rebellious
MUTUAL	LAMUTU	Possessed in common
OBTAIN	BNATOI	Get; acquire
OMINOUSLY	SYMONOIUL	Threateningly
OPTIMIST	MSITTIOP	One who always expects a favorable outcome
PERIL	PLERI	Danger
PERPETUAL	LAPPUETRE	Lasting forever
PHILANTHROPY	HILOPAYHTNPR	Giving charitable donations or aid
PRECISELY	CERPLEYIS	Exactly
PRECLUDED	LREDUPDEC	Prevented; made impossible by previous action
PRELUDE	EPDRLUE	Event or action preceding a more important one
PRODIGY	GYORPDI	Person with exceptional talents
PROXY	XRYOP	Person authorized to act for another
QUALMS	MALQSU	Issues causing uneasiness
REGIMENTATION	NEMTNOREGITIA	Uniformity and discipline
RENDEZVOUS	DEESZRUVON	Prearranged meeting
REPENTANT	TTEEPRANN	Feeling sorry for a wrong-doing

Cheaper By The Dozen Word List Continued

REPRIMAND	MDNERIRPA	A scolding, punishment or correction for doing something wrong
REPROBATES	SBEARPORET	Morally unprincipled people
RHETORICAL	THORCIRELA	Only one or no answer is expected
RIDICULE	CDIILREU	Make fun of
SIMULTANEOUS	TANSOUEMLISU	At the same time
SUBSEQUENT	QBSSEUUTEN	Following in order
SUBTLE	UBSETL	Not immediately obvious
SULLEN	NLEUSL	Showing ill-humor or resentment
SUPPLICATION	LTCOIPIPNAUS	Prayer; humble begging
SURGEONS	UEOSSNRG	Doctors who perform operations
SURREPTITIOUS	OUISIRUSPETTR	Performed or acquired by secret means
TACITLY	LCYITTA	Without speaking
TOLERATE	ROLEETTA	Allow without opposing
ULTIMATE	AIMETTLU	Final; best or most extreme example of its kind
UNANIMOUSLY	MLYONUASUIN	In complete agreement
UNREQUITED	QERTEDNUIU	Not returned
VERACITY	YCAVRETI	Truthfulness
VERGED	GVDREE	Came to the edge of
VICINITY	NIIYTVIC	Neighborhood; area
VITALITY	LTAIVYTI	Energy

VOCABULARY WORD SEARCH *Cheaper By The Dozen*

Words are placed backwards, forward, diagonally, up and down. Words listed below are included in the maze. Circle the hidden vocabulary words in the maze.

```
E V I T A I C E R P P A Y L T I C A T A
R X R L V J D V V C F H U C N F L S H D
E D T E D U L E R P Z R C A E O T P I M
P R T R T F E R O C I T Y U V R S N M O
R D G I I F J A D D M J S C N G N F Z N
I P T H S C Q C P M S U G U O O V A S I
M P H D X A A I U L D K T S C D C M U S
A U L T I M A T E H Y L S U O N I M O H
N L T L F R I Y E X L R O O A A N E R E
D T I B C N E C O M E U B I F L T L C D
E N Y S O E F R I Q S R B G P I E I I N
G E R U N G P R O D I G Y A C A R D D D
R R S O C R K N W M C N W T D S V F U H
E E M V E E N Y P E E E D N G U E R L N
V G L Z D M N L K N R P E O A L N A E F
D I A E E E I C L T P G E C L L E U L Z
J L U D D E O V T A A D F R L E S G T L
J L Q N D M D O C I L E R L I N N H B L
J E G E N V I T A L I T Y P E L C T U Q
B B C R C O N V I C T I O N D O R Y S H
```

ADMONISHED	CONVENT	FORGO	MUTINOUS	SUBTLE
AGENDA	CONVICTION	FRAUGHT	MUTUAL	SULLEN
AILING	DILEMMA	GALL	OMINOUSLY	TACITLY
ALIAS	DIRE	IMPLIED	PERIL	ULTIMATE
APPRECIATIVE	DOCILE	INDOLENT	PRECISELY	VERACITY
APTITUDE	DORY	INNOCUOUS	PRELUDE	VERGED
AWE	EMERGE	INTERVENE	PRODIGY	VITALITY
BELLIGERENT	ENSUE	IRKED	PROXY	
CAUCUS	ENTAIL	LUDICROUS	QUALMS	
CONCEDED	EXTRICATE	LURID	RENDEZVOUS	
CONTAGIOUS	FEROCITY	MOCK	REPRIMAND	

ANSWER KEY VOCABULARY WORD SEARCH *Cheaper By The Dozen*

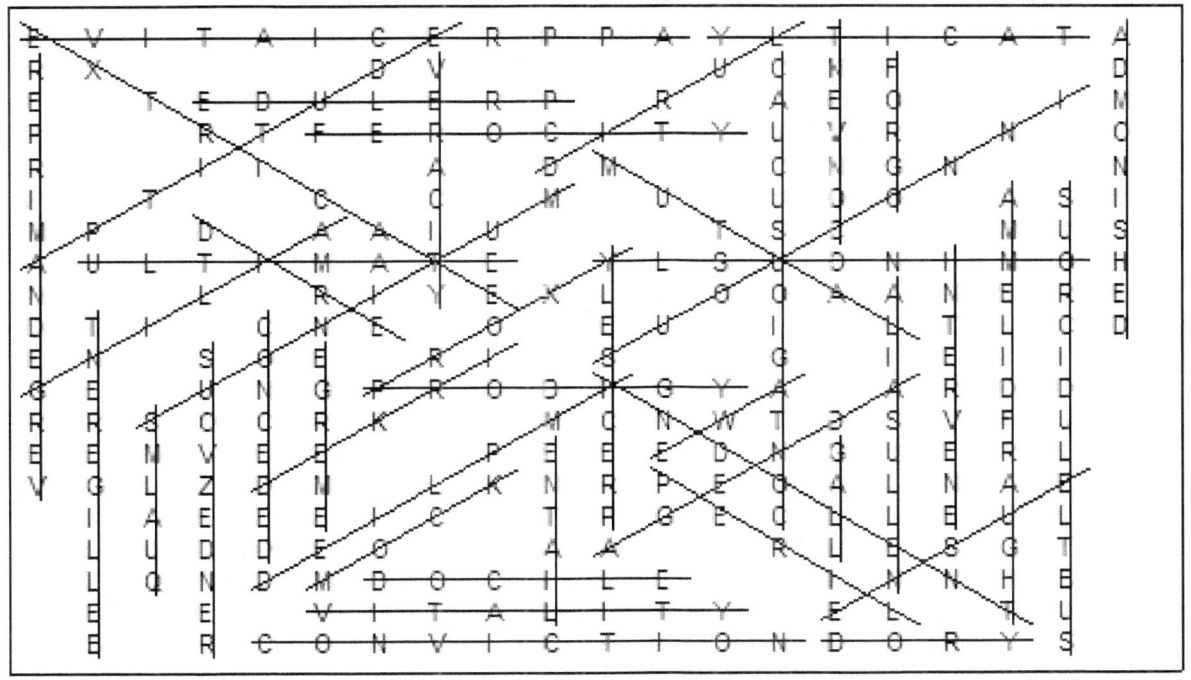

VOCABULARY CROSSWORD *Cheaper By The Dozen*

VOCABULARY CROSSWORD CLUES *Cheaper By The Dozen*

ACROSS
1 Person authorized to act for another
3 Ability
8 Demonstrate or point out
10 Without speaking
13 An emotion of respect and wonder tinged with fear
18 List of things to be done
20 Noisy uproar and confusion
22 Obedient; submissive to management
23 Irritated; annoyed
26 Causing shock or horror
27 Showing ill-humor or resentment
28 Imitation; false
29 An assumed name
30 Accompanied

DOWN
1 Event or action preceding a more important one
2 Threateningly
3 Find out
4 Unavoidable; going to happen no matter what
5 Final
6 Release from entanglement
7 Dislike intensely
9 Terrible; disastrous
11 Bestowed or given as an honor
12 A scolding, punishment or correction for doing something wrong
14 Self-assertiveness
15 Issues causing uneasiness
16 Lazy
17 Neighborhood; area
18 Ill; sick
19 Small, narrow, flat-bottomed boat
21 Truthfulness
24 Not immediately obvious
25 Possessed in common

VOCABULARY CROSSWORD ANSWER KEY *Cheaper By The Dozen*

VOCABULARY MATCHING 1 *Cheaper By The Dozen*

____ 1. RHETORICAL   A. Kind; charitable

____ 2. OBTAIN   B. Ill; sick

____ 3. VERGED   C. Harmless

____ 4. INNOCUOUS   D. Things (usually negative) implied or suggested

____ 5. INNUENDOES   E. Give up

____ 6. CAPITULATED   F. Obedient; submissive to management

____ 7. INDOLENT   G. Neighborhood; area

____ 8. PERIL   H. Get; acquire

____ 9. COINCIDE   I. Came to the edge of

____ 10. PHILANTHROPY   J. Lazy

____ 11. VICINITY   K. Not returned

____ 12. PROXY   L. One who always expects a favorable outcome

____ 13. FORGO   M. Morally unprincipled people

____ 14. REPRIMAND   N. Yielded; gave in

____ 15. REPROBATES   O. A scolding, punishment or correction for doing something wrong

____ 16. OPTIMIST   P. Only one or no answer is expected

____ 17. AILING   Q. Person authorized to act for another

____ 18. BENEVOLENT   R. Danger

____ 19. DOCILE   S. To happen at the same time

____ 20. UNREQUITED   T. Giving charitable donations or aid

VOCABULARY MATCHING 2 *Cheaper By The Dozen*

____ 1. CONFERRED   A. Self-assertiveness

____ 2. AILING   B. Noisy uproar and confusion

____ 3. GALL   C. Tending to spread from one to another

____ 4. CONTAGIOUS   D. Dislike intensely

____ 5. BEDLAM   E. Lazy

____ 6. IMPLORED   F. Find out

____ 7. PERIL   G. Begged for urgently

____ 8. DETEST   H. A scolding, punishment or correction for doing something wrong

____ 9. ASCERTAIN   I. Ill; sick

____ 10. ENSCONCED   J. Showing ill-humor or resentment

____ 11. DILEMMA   K. Unavoidable; going to happen no matter what

____ 12. DEBACLE   L. Danger

____ 13. CALLIOPE   M. Settled securely

____ 14. INNOCUOUS   N. Musical keyboard fitted with steam whistles

____ 15. INEVITABLE   O. Rebellious

____ 16. SULLEN   P. Harmless

____ 17. ATROCIOUS   Q. Exceptionally bad

____ 18. MUTINOUS   R. Disaster

____ 19. REPRIMAND   S. A situation requiring a choice

____ 20. INDOLENT   T. Bestowed or given as an honor

VOCABULARY MATCHING ANSWER KEYS *Cheaper By The Dozen*

	MATCH 1	MATCH 2
1	P	T
2	H	I
3	I	A
4	C	C
5	D	B
6	N	G
7	J	L
8	R	D
9	S	F
10	T	M
11	G	S
12	Q	R
13	E	N
14	O	P
15	M	K
16	L	J
17	B	Q
18	A	O
19	F	H
20	K	E

www.ingramcontent.com/pod-product-compliance
Lightning Source LLC
LaVergne TN
LVHW081536060526
838200LV00048B/2097